Hindu at Heart

HINDU AT HEART

Education, Faith, and What it Means to Belong in America

INDU VISWANATHAN, Ed.D.

TSPA

THE SELF PUBLISHING AGENCY

Indu Viswanathan, Ed.D.
Hindu at Heart: Education, Faith, and What it Means to Belong in America

Briarcliff Press
Copyright 2025 by Indu Viswanathan
First Edition

Softcover ISBN: 979-8-9945356-1-5
Hardcover ISBN: 979-8-9945356-0-8
eBook ISBN: 979-8-9945356-2-2

Book Design | Danna Steele
Editor | Amy Tyler
Publishing Management | TSPA The Self Publishing Agency, Inc.

For Amma and Appa.
Everything I am is because of you.

For Rahul and Ajay.
Everything I am is for you, my darlings.

TABLE OF CONTENTS

Preface

Fall 1987

I can taste the fire on my tongue.

A rage of words and emotions courses through my system as I stare at the image of "India," spread over two pages of our seventh-grade social studies textbook. Hot tears collect behind my eyes. In all these years, the topics of India and Hinduism have not come up in school. It's been my personal secret world, safely hidden in the magical portal of home, on the not-rich side of Briarcliff Manor, a tiny village in Westchester County, New York. We've lived there since I was a baby. And I've had the privacy of entire summers spent in India, all the way on the other side of the planet, with my beautiful, generous family.

The one exception was when Amma came to visit my first-grade class in her sari and talked about Ganesha and our temples and holidays.

Scratch that.

There was another time when Hinduism and India came up. How could I forget? A few years ago, when *The Temple of Doom* came out. A dark cave filled with dirty Kali worshippers as the Hindu priest grinned creepily at the audience while blood dripped down his arm from the freshly scavenged monkey brain he held in his hand. The good Christian Indian riding on the top of the train with Indiana Jones, cheerfully telling him in adorable Indian English how he drinks the blood of Christ every Sunday. It was your basic "Aren't those Hindus scary savages, and aren't Indian Christian converts adorable and relatable?" message. I was afraid kids at school would ask me about that. But I was quiet and nerdy and didn't talk to many people. My guess was that instead of saying it directly to me, people probably just silently thought it *at* me.

Me, age 11

Other than that, there'd been no mention of Hinduism or India.

Until now, in seventh grade social studies class.

I look down at the image again. My vision is framed by the edges of my luxurious new perm and the rim of my translucent beige plastic glasses. A woman in a torn, dirty sari is ambling down a dirt road, carrying a clay pot filled with water on her head, hips swung to one side, as exotic women do. On her right is a mud hut, on her left a colorful garbage heap piled high past her head. She shares the dirt road with some emaciated cows.

"INDIA," the top left corner of the page announces.

I can see my classmates smelling the image. The dirt, the heat, the squalor … the exotic, disgusting, pitiable odor of the "developing world."

Mr. Gross is at his desk; its solid oak authority angled at the front of the classroom next to the chalkboard. I hear my heart beating loudly over my classmates' silent downward gaze. Do they hear it? My braces suddenly feel very heavy on my teeth. The armpits of my Joyce Leslie sweater with the geometric print are beginning to swim in puberty-and-injustice sweat, heat travels up my neck. I have never spoken out about anything before. I am shy at school. The well-behaved, rule-following, firstborn child of immigrants.

But I have grown up in a home inspired by inquiry. I have been raised in a community of Hindu scientists who are pioneers in their fields of innovation while also holding deep reverence for the Divine. I have grown up immersed in the Hindu spirit of exploration and wonder, of dialogue and voice.

I stand up. The sound of the metal legs with the rubber feet pushing against the porcelain tile floor.

"This is not *my* India."

Mr. Gross looks at me, eyes slightly widened, pushing his glasses back up into position. His mouth expands into a gentle smile.

"Why don't you tell us about *your* India?"

Summer 2023

I land at San Francisco International Airport in the early afternoon and rent a sassy red Honda Civic. I drive east, past rolling mustard-hued hills dotted with industrial windmill farms listlessly spinning electricity. Jazz singer Madeleine Peyroux croons "Dance Me to the End of Love," through the speakers. My thoughts settle as I focus on the task ahead of me.

In many ways, this is a culminating moment for me. It has been almost 40 years since I was a seventh grader speaking out in class about how our social studies textbook misrepresented India and Hinduism. It's been over 20 years since I became a public school teacher. It's been nearly four years since I finished my doctoral program in curriculum and teaching, where I learned to listen deeply and with humility and to understand how immigrant communities make meaning of and advocate for their children's education.

And now, I am here in California, about to interview a dozen Hindu American families. I imagine stories of injustice and frustration about public education and about how disenfranchised and marginalized Hindu immigrant parents feel in an unfamiliar system. I remind myself not to be swayed by preconceived narratives. And it's a good thing I do, because what I hear during those two weeks in the Bay Area is nothing like the stories I had imagined.

I'm getting ahead of myself! I should explain why I went to California, why I felt it was so important to go there and meet these families.

Every six years, the California Department of Education conducts a comprehensive review of its curricular materials, incorporating public input into the process. Among the materials under scrutiny are textbooks produced by private corporations, publishers you might remember from your school days, like Houghton Mifflin and McGraw-Hill. The practice of entering public testimony into the record as part of reviewing materials used in tax-funded schools, illustrates the intricate relationship between American democracy, public education, and the business sector.

In 2005, Hindu Americans entered public testimony with the Board of Education, disputing proposed changes and representations of Hinduism in school textbooks. In 2017, over 800 Hindu American students and parents traveled from the Bay Area and San Diego to Sacramento to testify about the representations of Hinduism in their school curricula. Hindu American advocacy groups also showed up, not only from local chapters but at the national level. This was the largest group of people that had ever shown up to testify before the department. It was, without exaggeration, a historic event for California and Hindu Americans. (Since then, scholars and journalists have represented both the 2005 and 2017 events on university websites, scholarly publications, and news reports.) Ominous phrases like "Hindutva deluge," "hydra-headed Hindutva," "saffron assault," were used to describe the Hindu Americans who organized and traveled to California, presenting them as Hindu extremists. Progressive media, scholars, and activists express concerns that an alleged militant Hindu supremacy is infiltrating American society, operating in opposition to the ideals of social justice and progressivism. It is linked with the bogeyman of Hindu nationalism in India, which is compared and equated with Christian nationalism in the United States. This feeds the contemporary discourse about Hindu Americans, particularly immigrants, that looms large in the progressive American imagination.

A part of my research is to find out if any of this is actually true. Are these Hindu Americans looking to silence pluralist representations of Hinduism? Are they anti-intellectual religious extremists unwilling to confront uncomfortable, established truths about their religion, as they are often described?

And, so, I travel to the Bay Area to interview 22 of those 800 people who testified in 2017. I spend ten days in the region, staying with the families who insist I "come home" and not stay in a hotel. In Hinduism, we have a practice of *atithi devo bhava* (the guest is the equivalent of God). I am the grateful recipient of this generosity everywhere I go. I receive endless cups of delicious chai, homemade meals from across the regions of India, and the warmest receptions from all family members every time I enter a home. Apart from a few folks, I have never met any of these people before. For 10 days, I immerse myself in their stories, sometimes spending five or six hours in just one home. A conversation with one person lasts at least an hour. Together, we trace back from childhood through the journey leading up to 2017, all the way to the present. I am struck by the variety of stories and perspectives, the passion and sense of purpose, the realization that this was actually a historic moment for the Hindu American community, and that most people, most Hindu Americans, don't even know it happened.

I ask each participant if any scholar, including the movement's leaders, has ever contacted them to understand their perspective. Everyone responds with no. No scholar had ever contacted a single one of them to interview them, not even the movement's leaders. As far as they knew, no scholar had reached out to any of the 800 people who appeared in Sacramento that day to find out if the claims made about them had any substance.

I was the first scholar to sit with any of them and listen to their stories.

You may have been in a situation where someone misrepresents you or your ideas in ways that are so far removed from what you actually believe that it's almost impossible to sort out how to speak across the gap. Social media has certainly multiplied the effect of this kind of phenomenon, but it has always existed. When someone misrepresents you, when they broadcast a version of you that is so far from who you know yourself to be, it's easy for feelings of injustice, silencing, and frustration to creep in. You may have experienced how easily one incident of misrepresentation can snowball into complete misunderstandings, where walls are erected and suddenly you find yourself the "other," and it doesn't matter what you say, because no one is listening. People have decided that your words lack integrity.

Or, if you're lucky, you've felt that sweet relief wash over your senses when someone *does* listen, with care, real attention, and an open mind. You know how an act of true listening not only creates a sweet connection; it can dissolve misunderstanding and create harmony.

Listening is at the heart of this book. Listening with the intention of really understanding another perspective. Listening to understand what is happening. Listening with lightness.

Listening to Hindu Americans outside of my echo chamber led me to write this book. When I decided to switch fields and go into education over 25 years ago, I joined a master's program that was committed to inclusion. That was important to me, as a Hindu American. After I got my degree and entered the world of education, I experienced two related phenomena clearly (and sometimes uncomfortably). First, despite the best of intentions, social justice spaces weren't always designed for people to listen without preconceptions. And second, when someone *did* listen with a truly open mind, humor and humility, it felt like magic and settled the energy in the room.

When I went back to pursue a doctorate 15 years later, I learned that becoming a scholar means coming face to face with how little you know. In fact, I learned that being a scholar is actually a practice in humility and lifelong learning. At the same time, I encountered the concept of the "scholar activist," which I first assumed was a way of embracing the higher purpose of learning and knowledge to uplift society. What I learned over the course of graduate school is that *scholar* and *activist* are not really compatible. An activist has an important role in sociopolitics. To fulfill that role they must adopt a specific perspective, a position they've taken on about what is right and what is wrong, what counts as truth and what doesn't. The activist's job is to hold people in a space until the people around them agree or at least accept that their perspective is the righteous or the moral perspective. A scholar's role is to question and be in wonder about the world around them, about what they hold to be true and especially about what has become truth through consensus in the intellectual class. It requires a great deal of humility to question what they even think they already know. But this is the wellspring of innovation, development, and intellectual achievement.

This is also the case for the educator. Our role as educators is to teach our students how to examine how they think about the world, not tell them what they must believe about it. As a teacher educator, I would hear emergent teachers in my social studies methods course ask me, "Why did no one, before now, teach me to question what I think I know? To ask myself *why* I believe what I believe?"

Of course, this is all well and good in theory. Practice is always more … colorful … and this part of my journey coincided with the aftermath of Donald Trump's election. I saw Hindu Americans engaging in political rhetoric that didn't make any sense to me. It didn't align with what I understood to be a Dharmic outlook, which is pluralist and inclusive and about taking right action in the world, not fear-mongering and othering. I also saw connections being made in the media and by Hindu Americans on either side of the aisle between Indian and American politics. I couldn't make sense of it and began talking to my parents, who immigrated from India to New York in the 1960s. They had always modeled Dharma and openly and avidly supported equality across all markers. As I lay down my righteousness and embraced humility in my listening, I began to understand things in a much more complex way. At the same time, I started seeing media stories and survey studies—often conducted by fellow Hindu Americans— that weren't necessarily looking to understand *why* people were making the choices they were. Everywhere I looked, I saw assumptions that were based on the media rehashing false parallels over and over again until they appeared factual! I didn't see any significant attempt to understand or listen to Hindu Americans. So, I decided to listen—at a deep, sometimes uncomfortable, level—to other Hindus in this country whose politics were very different from mine. I stopped assuming that I could understand them based on their most polemic or politicized expression. For over six years, I have been listening with an open mind to their stories, their fears, their aspirations, their worldviews to better understand how to decode and make sense of what they are saying from *their perspective.*

It didn't take a lot of digging to understand the fundamental role American public education played in how Hinduism and Hindus were imagined by the American public, including by many Hindu Americans themselves. Looking back, had I not been wrestling with some version of this myself in the decades since Mr. Gross's class?

The dominant narrative in American K-12 education is that Hinduism is incompatible with democracy. I know this sounds like an exaggerated claim, especially to people who aren't that familiar with the subject. How could our schools teach something that biased? Why would they? Even now, well into the 21st century?

Unfortunately, it's not an exaggeration. It is so deeply baked into what is taught that you need a decoder ring to understand the hidden curriculum. It's one of those things that you can't unsee once you see it.

Figure 1. Front page of *The Washington Herald* (February 21, 1923).

As I continued to listen to Hindu American families, I began to see another important pattern come into focus: Hindu Americans are actively participating in and upholding democratic values and civic responsibilities through their engagement with our public school system. And public school teachers are listening with care and compassion to understand and learn.

When we put our attention only toward what isn't fair or working well, we miss seeing that there is a fuller picture or grounded reality that is both hopeful and significant.

This book is written as a resource for Hindu American families with children in K–12 schools, and for the educators and community members who engage with them. My intention is to provide context, history, and language that make inter-group dialogues more generative, meaningful, and transparent. I begin from the belief that, by and large, Americans are fundamentally good people who want to do right by their neighbors, their students, and their teachers. In my view, every reader of this book, and every person represented within it, is a protagonist in the American story, living, imagining, and shaping our complex national narrative in times of turmoil and peace, both of which are inevitable and are sometimes concurrent.

Introduction

These stories speak to our collective striving
toward a more perfect union. From the
beginning, America had to be—and still
remains to be—crafted.[1]

– Frances K. Pohl, *Framing America*

This book is not a curriculum guide on Hinduism, and it is not a religious text. I am not a scholar of religion—I am a Hindu American educator and parent and a scholar of education.

Hinduism is not just a religion in the ways that the three Western religions—Christianity, Judaism, and Islam—are. Trying to understand Hinduism through the Western concept of religion is like trying to describe a Broadway musical using an inch tape. The tool doesn't help us understand the subject. You might hear some Hindus describe their faith as a *way of life* but even that, I believe, doesn't really do it justice. Hinduism is an inquiry tradition, a way of understanding our mind, our location in the world, and how to navigate it. The original name of Hinduism is Sanātana Dharma. Sanātana means eternal and Dharma loosely translates into righteous action. (A favorite definition of mine is that Dharma is that which brings us all closer together, that unites society.) Sanātana Dharma is a living, breathing system.

What I offer here is insight and inquiry grounded in lived experience, field research, and scholarly reflection. This is not a dense academic monograph; it is an accessible, thoughtful companion for those who want to better understand how Hindu American families are situated within—and can contribute to—the evolving story of K-12 American public education.

For centuries, the way Hindus and Hinduism have been studied and represented in the U.S. hasn't included sincere dialogue with Hindus themselves. American textbooks, media, and public perception regularly misrepresent our perspectives and our lives, to the point where these representations are just … absurd!

Right before the pandemic, I was invited by a group of Hindu students at Rutgers University to conduct an interactive workshop on Hinduphobia. This particular group was composed largely of international graduate students who had grown up in India. Inspired by my recent reading of Vamsee Juluri's *Rearming Hinduism*, I decided to have a little fun and do a kind of live experiment. A few minutes into the session, I read aloud the following passage from the book describing infamous Hinduism expert Wendy Doniger's claims about Hindus and monsoons:

> The Hinduism expert tells us something about our weather too.
>
> According to Doniger, the monsoon's "violence" and "uncertainty" create a perennial psychological

condition in us that gives us our beliefs about our whimsical and violent gods. This is not a pop theory from the 19th century colonial fantasy to explain tropical tribal superstition. This is the present. This is the cutting-edge of leading Hinduism expertise.

Let us begin with this view of the monsoon. For us, the monsoon is not a deadly storm like an itch in jealous Zeus's beard. To anyone who knows India, or the Hindus, really knows us, that is; for someone who comes to us and opens their eyes and ears and listens and watches, and gets off their own solitary mind-fantasy, the monsoon is not about violence, but merely a blessing and a festival.

Think of Kalidasa. Read the classics. Watch Lagaan. Watch a thousand Bollywood movies. The Indian mind does not associate the monsoon with violence.

The only meaning we have for the monsoon is that it marks the return of everything to life. It is relief from the heat. It is children laughing, peacocks dancing, the sound of frogs, plants growing, life renewed, hope.

And our gods too are like our monsoon. They give us life. We welcome their return, again and again.

We do not think of our gods as capricious.

Our god stories are totally about causality, karma, reason. No one is whimsical; even Narada, we tell ourselves, is only seemingly an itinerant trouble-maker. He sets things in motion that will lead to ultimate good.

Our stories do not tell us our gods are irrationally violent. Forceful, yes, but not without reason. Our sensibility does not teach us to fear them as much as to trust them, worship them, and believe in their fairness; even when we sometimes complain. A devotional view of the divine does not come from a position of uncertainty and fear.

It appears to be a foreign thing.

Maybe it's…their weather."[2]

We were sitting in a circle of chairs in a lecture hall on campus. When I finished reading, there was silence. I opened the floor up for discussion, letting them know that there were no wrong responses. (I was very aware that the students from India might need me to give permission for them to speak up and even disagree with what I had read, as that is not the norm in many Indian classrooms.)

What followed was a flood of incredulity.

"What on earth is Wendy Doniger talking about? "

"Afraid of the monsoon?"

"We dance for the monsoon. We pray for the monsoon!"

"There are songs and poems written about the monsoon! We love the monsoon!"

Having lived in Mumbai for a couple of years when my children were very little, I could completely understand how stupefied they were. Monsoon is magical. As Juluri notes, Hindus' relationship with the seasons, including monsoon season, is encoded in Hindu culture, symbolism, literature, art, oral histories.

Doniger's claims about Indian Hindus' relationship with the monsoon were so absurd—so far removed from anything actual Indian Hindus know—that it was hard to find the words to express *how* off the mark she is.

Of course, there may be Indian Hindus who don't like the monsoon, who don't like how undrivable the roads are, how mold grows on upholstery, how buildings need to be repainted, and the day-to-day inconveniences.

But imagine centering just those voices and using them as substantiating evidence of Doniger's claims about the Hindu relationship with monsoon. We wouldn't necessarily describe this as intellectually honest, would we?

And yet this is what happens all the time!

Academics, journalists, and media producers often cherry pick voices of Hindus who echo non-Hindu perspectives about Hinduism. These Hindus add an aura of authenticity, not only through their identities but by contributing personal anecdotes that fit nicely into the dominant narrative. While these anecdotes may, indeed, be authentic examples, they are offered to and internalized by the public as *generalizable*, as if these stories are representative of the entire Hindu experience and Hinduism, itself.

The danger of a stereotype is that it is not always a lie. The danger of a stereotype is that it is often a tiny sliver of truth that is decontextualized and magnified and presented over and over again as the entire truth, until the mere suggestion of any other information or context appears absurd, false, and even, as in the case of Hindus, an attempt to squash the truth.

In recent years, the deleterious impact of squashing viewpoint diversity on American campuses has come into painful focus. Much of the conversation about free speech is focused on provocative and harmful speech. But the deeper issue lies in the deliberate suppression of diverse perspectives, often on the basis of identity, undermining the very purpose of academia. This degrades an environment that is meant to value interrogating popular narratives and foregone conclusions. Academic consensus, when it deliberately silences viewpoint diversity, is not scientific or in pursuit of the truth or the betterment of society. It is a weapon. That is precisely what we are seeing on campuses today. Alarmingly, that weaponization is being justified.

The weaponization of academic consensus stifles intellectual curiosity and contributes to a generation of students conditioned to avoid and even feel "harmed" by dissenting viewpoints. Jonathan Haidt and Greg Lukianoff explore this phenomenon in *The Coddling of the American Mind*. I have seen this degradation transpire throughout my own lifetime. I see how anger (however justified) has infiltrated campuses and exhausted the individual and collective nervous system, making it feel unsafe to consider other, new, disruptive information. However, I believe we can course correct.

Genuine inquiry is a brave and humble and achievable endeavor, not a campaign of righteous indignation. It is not just about the right to speak. It is about the responsibility to listen.

This is not a collection of stories about the Hindu struggle to fit into American society through the public education system. It is not about immigrant assimilation or an examination of Hindu-American *identity*. I did not want to offer you a book about struggling. Instead, I explore how Hindu Americans are collectively striving "for a more perfect union,"[3] as outlined in the Preamble to the U.S. Constitution, through our public education system. Every American community that has not been fairly represented in our democracy has participated in striving, and, often, K-12 education sits at the heart of it. That striving is beautiful—even though it has often been fraught or frustrating—because it is premised on speaking bravely and listening humbly, of sincere connection and respect. And in that striving we learn so much about each other. Our worlds expand!

That striving towards expansiveness is what drives this book. I examine the Hindu American experience in ways that haven't sufficiently been explored by educational scholars. I celebrate the important relationship between public school teachers and communities. And I invite you to discover with me how learning about these Hindu American perspectives can lead to greater and different understandings of other minority groups. And how all of this contributes to the great experiment of American democracy.

This might come as a shock to some readers, but since the inception of the common school system (the predecessor of today's public school system) in the newly independent

United States, American education has propagated a story that Hinduism stands in opposition to ideals of democracy. This story is premised upon the assumption that Hinduism is immoral, irrational, and irredeemable, a portrayal that originated from colonial and missionary reports from India. These reports inherently excluded the perspectives of Hindus themselves, and were, by their very nature, self-serving in their agenda. (This approach of *testimonial injustice* delegitimizes Hindu knowledge of our own tradition and people. It centers the outsider, Western gaze and interpretation as authoritative and was also taken up in academic studies of Hinduism and India. This approach continues to this day.) The idea that Hinduism is allegedly incompatible with democracy persists to this day, creating a permission structure that validates the chronic erasing, silencing, and misrepresenting of Hindu American perspectives, voices, and hearts.

I am a product of American public education and a parent of former public-school students. I have also spent over 20 years in various roles in the field of public education, including as a public-school teacher, the research director of an educational non-profit, a teacher educator, and a scholar of education. I think a lot about schools and kids! I am also a Hindu American—the child of immigrants who arrived in the 1960s—who grew up in the public education system and raised two Hindu American children. I have spent years studying the chasm between the representations of Hinduism in K-12 American public education and the history of Hindus and Hinduism. I think it is important for people to understand this gap, but I think it is just as important to amplify solutions that are already happening on the ground. How can we learn from these examples as we move forward? What are the implications for American education?

You might think me romantic or idealistic, but if we look at the purpose of education, of scholarship, of journalism, the idea is to move us closer to the truth so that we can have a clearer way of understanding ourselves and the world around us. What is good practice as we inquire towards the truth? Hindus have a very powerful practice called *purva paksha*—before you get into a debate or question someone's ideas, you ensure that you can articulate their ideas and position accurately and with intellectual honesty. This has informed my research process for this book and opened up my mind beyond my own biases and assumptions.

This collection of stories and essays illuminates *and* challenges prevailing narratives that have demonized Hinduism in American schools. Through personal narratives, historical analysis, and interviews with Hindu American families, my goal is to contextualize and offer a tool for Hindu Americans working in collaboration with our public school system. I provide a nuanced history of Hinduism in American education, contextualize the role of American education in shaping American society, and equip readers with language and perspectives to better understand Hindu American experiences in the context of K-12 education and immigration. Driven by a passion to shape a more inclusive American democracy centered on pluralism, I weave my own personal experiences and stories of the Hindu Americans I interviewed between essays about American education. My larger goal extends beyond these pages. I want to create spaces for honest, compassionate intergroup dialogue. My goal is to leave readers feeling expanded and inspired that we can learn and imagine something new about American democracy by understanding and engaging with Hindu American acts and attitudes of pluralism.

I invite readers to delve with me into the roots of fixed narratives about Hindu Americans and endeavor to move beyond them. Let us discover new, more generative ways of representing Hinduism in our public schools. And let us consider the contributions that Hindu Americans and Hinduism can make to a reimagined American democracy founded on pluralism.

These chapters represent my experiment and experiences in listening deeply, letting go of preconceived notions, laughing at the absurd, and applying our learning beyond the Hindu American experience. It is for any American who wants to learn why you might believe what you believe about Hindus and Hinduism. But it is also for people who want to understand how and why even well-intended humanitarian education can get it so wrong and what we can do about it. So many Americans today have a deep longing to feel safe and heard and understood, beyond the labeling and canceling and fracturing that has proliferated in recent years and seems to have calcified deep chasms between us. This book recognizes the power of deep listening with the purpose of understanding. It honors how we yearn for people to listen for what we mean and not just hear what we say. What can happen when we listen to the hearts of people whom we think are very different from us?

This book moves between history, lived experience, and critical reflection to surface how Hindus and Hinduism have been represented in the U.S. public education system. Each chapter builds on the last to deepen our understanding of how these representations shape the public imagination, impact students and families, and intersect with the civic and cultural landscape of American democracy through our public education system.

Throughout this book, you will see me using the term K-12 education. This is shorthand for kindergarten through 12th grade, or the aggregate of early, elementary, and secondary education. You'll also see me refer to this as school; I will differentiate clearly when I am talking about higher education, i.e., college and beyond. Within each chapter, you'll find glimpses of Hindu Americans whose lived experiences reflect the theoretical and historical discussions. These profiles are not representative of the entire community—or even the entire interview—nor are they meant to be. They offer moments of humanity, contradiction, resilience, depth, and often humor. Together, the chapters and stories in this book form a mosaic—a composite of a community asking to be understood on its own terms while also striving to offer something sincere and profound to the larger experiment of American democracy.

At its heart, this book is an invitation. An invitation to listen, to reflect, and to participate in shaping a more honest, inclusive, and pluralistic public sphere—one in which Hindu Americans are not only present but fully heard and meaningfully engaged.

How to Use This Book

This book is designed to help Hindu American families, students, and communities engage more consciously and effectively with the U.S. public education system and to support educators and allies who wish to better understand *why* they believe what they believe about Hinduism and the lived experiences, concerns, and perspectives of Hindu Americans in

K–12 schools. It is meant to be read, discussed, and used as a springboard for meaningful dialogue and action in schools, communities, and in the public sphere. Suggested ways to use this book include:

Host a community reading circle: Invite students and families to read and discuss one chapter at a time, in person, in small groups.

Gift it to a teacher, journalist, or policymaker: Share it with people who influence public understandings of Hinduism and Hindu Americans.

Use it in teacher education: Include it in teacher preparation or professional development workshops on pluralism and representation.

Draw from it in journalism and media work: Journalists and public commentators can use its historical and lived-experience insights to avoid stereotypes and broaden coverage.

Incorporate excerpts into advocacy: Bring relevant passages to curriculum reviews, school board meetings, or community forums to ground discussions in evidence and lived realities.

Integrate it into community education: Use chapters and vignettes in Hindu Sunday schools, cultural classes, and youth leadership programs.

Facilitate interfaith and intercommunity dialogues: Use the book as a starting point for conversations about representation, democracy, and belonging across traditions.

Revisit it over time: Return to chapters as public debates evolve or as new questions arise in education, media, or policy.

Sankalpa (Intention)

August 1980

"It seems that your daughter is not ready for kindergarten. I asked her to draw a house, and she drew it upside down. She seems a little confused. Maybe it's because she's bilingual."

I don't say anything.

Amma knows that while I'm usually silent in public, an avalanche of words will come spilling out of me in the car. On the drive home, she asks,

"Why did you draw the house upside down, Induma?"

"So he could see from there!!"

At four and three-quarter years old, I am shy around strangers, especially serious, mustachioed school psychologists in suburban New York. Sitting across from him at the large wooden desk, wearing my smocked dress, my favorite ribbon barrettes in my hair, I had done my best work: I wanted to make sure he would see the house right side up from where he was sitting.

Amma turns our honey-colored Dodge Dart around and heads back to Todd Elementary School. If you knew Amma, you'd understand how remarkable this is. While she is fierce about her children, she is no outspoken, in-your-face tiger mom. Her energy is more like a deer. But she is not about to let me be held back a year because of the school psychologist's assumptions about me and his lack of curiosity in understanding my perspective.

Amma speaks to the school principal, who listens to my immigrant mom with her British Indian accent, and I begin kindergarten the next fall.

Intention, Impact, and Assumptions

Let's talk for a moment about intention and impact.

Have you heard (or maybe even used) the phrase "Impact is greater than intent"? The idea here is that our intentions are immaterial if our actions lead to some hurt or harm. We must hold ourselves accountable (or we are held accountable) because our impact matters most. If you step on my foot by accident, my foot hurts, even if you didn't mean to step on it.

This approach toward social interaction has gained widespread popularity, particularly in discussions about interpersonal communication, social justice, classrooms, and even in the workplace. The goal of this principle is to encourage people to be more socially aware, more self-reflective, and to learn how to think outside of their own bubble.

But what happens when we hold a mirror up to this idea?

If impact is greater than intent, what is the *impact* of that principle?

In my world of interactions, I have noticed that "impact is greater than intent" is often held up as a chastisement, a slap on the wrist. The energy shifts away from dialogue, and it can quite suddenly become a lecture that seems to go in one direction—from the offended to the offender.

This isn't to say that we never need to be lectured. But certainly, intentions matter!

After all, isn't there a different implication about your relationship with someone if they step on your foot ... *on purpose*?

There are psychological implications of discarding or diminishing the value of intentions, both individually and socially. Devaluing intent can lead to over-blaming and over-punishing.[4] It can result in imputing hostile intent where there is none, increasing aggression and levels of conflict.[5] It is developmentally less mature to ignore intent.[6] Devaluing intent and overvaluing impact reduce nuance in moral judgement and fairness.[7]

In other words, our intentions matter a great deal.

Mind the Gap

Imagine that our intentions and our impact exist in two spheres. They're not fixed or solid, but more like gaseous, swirling spheres, floating in space. The spheres are assemblages of multiple things. Intentions include our sense of morality, our sense of self, our analytical lenses, our assumptions about things outside of just ourselves, about the world, society, government, etc. Impact encompasses facial expressions, actions, words, conversations, relationships.

When we feel the gap between our intention and our impact, when it is called to our attention, or we notice it, it can impact us in almost visceral ways. It can feel like a pinch because we want to be good, moral people in the world and not cause harm. Rather than thinking about the pinch as a punishment, as something we ought to be ashamed of, what would happen if we could embrace it as a wake-up call that can guide us toward greater alignment, as something that we can all learn from.

The pinch doesn't tell us that we need to be fixed; it's announcing that we are about to grow.

Sankalpa

In Hinduism, there is this idea of a *sankalpa*. A sankalpa is a strong, positive intention or resolve and can even be directly offered up as a declaration of purpose. There is a powerful energetic commitment that surfaces with something like this; it's not even always clear how it's going to unfold. We can even accept that mistakes may happen along the way, but our intention is higher than any individual action or misstep that we might think of as impact.

For the purpose of this conversation, let us hold that space between good intention and imperfect impact with grace, humility, and compassion. If you are reading this book, if you are like me, you are here to learn, to increase your self- and social awareness. It is only with grace, humility, and compassion (and humor) that we can actually create the space for that kind of growth as individuals and as a collective.

We are imperfect, and we're always going to be imperfect. If we see that space between impact and intention as a sacred space, or a cherished space where so much learning can happen, then there is hope. If there is hope and we can set down our hardened shields to defend our reputations as "good people," then our actions can be held a little bit more lightly as actions, and the effect of those actions will play out in many complex ways, beyond what we can comprehend (think butterfly effect). This is actually what the concept of karma implies, not revenge or a simple, obvious consequence. In other words, the impact is beyond our realm of control.

That isn't to say we don't take responsibility and take action for our impact in the world. But if that action is reflecting in that space between intention and impact, then we can learn to skillfully bring those things closer together, examining our assumptions, our ideas, our preconceived notions. Perhaps that is the feeling of being in integrity that we seek. I think all of us want to be in integrity, to feel integrated and not fractured.

Zooming out larger, beyond the individual path, we can even think about how the project of American democracy includes a layer of integration—integrating with each other in a way that's meaningful, open, and pluralist. I offer, humbly, that this a really powerful framework for us to use not just broadly in society but even in terms of what we model for our children at home and teach our children in schools.

Listening with Love

I believe that the longing to get things right exists because of love. Love wants us to be in alignment between intention and impact, between thought and action, not only because of our own integrity but because love connects us. Love is about relationships, love is about impact, love is about social harmony.

We can't be afraid of talking about love when we're talking about things like schools, democracy, society, and community. It's simply not effective.

I have also found, whether it is in personal relationships, in professional settings, in the classroom, even sometimes in tense social media interactions, that laughter and humor soften the space for grace to flourish. Grace allows us to develop greater social harmony, to understand that we might not be singing the same notes or have the same vocal range, but that we can still sing together.

My sankalpa is that we learn to hold grace for each other with love, humor, humility, and compassion beyond the pages of this book. And that this intention affords us the courage to move ourselves, our students, our children, and our learning communities back toward the viewpoint diversity that allows for authentic inquiry to happen.

Milind and Yagnee

You will have a community to stick by you.
You will always have that community, and
that community will help you be proud of
who you are and accept who you are instead
of going around and telling girls to take their
bindis off at school.

– Yagnee Makwana, about being Hindu
American today

August 2023

It's been three days since I first arrived in the East Bay. My hostess, Divya, graciously makes me fresh smoothies every morning with fruits picked from her backyard.

Ah, California!

I have already visited four different homes, shared generous, delicious meals with four different families, and interviewed five parents and five young Hindu Americans.

Now it is time for me to relocate to the South Bay with another welcoming family.

Moments after I arrive at my new host Akshay's home in San Jose, I find myself back in my red Civic with four teenage girls in the late afternoon heat. I am somewhat following Akshay in his minivan, which is packed with other assorted children. That's how it is sometimes, right? You show up at someone's house to conduct ethnographic research, they're in a completely different moment than what you could have anticipated, and suddenly you're driving to In-N-Out Burger with a gaggle of teenagers while listening to Taylor Swift.

I have never met these young women before, and they have never met me. But, somehow, we easily find ourselves in the middle of a conversation about music, pop culture, growing up, and parents. Then they ask,

"How old are you, anyway?"

"Well, my kids are 17 and 18. I'm probably older than most of your parents!"

"That's weird! You're … like us!"

I think I know what they mean. Their parents are all immigrants. And as much as I'd love to believe my preternatural youthfulness has outmatched my middle age, they're not talking about age. It's that I am also a child of Indian Hindu immigrants, that I can relate to some of their experiences of being a bridge between worlds. It's that I sound like them (well, maybe more New York than California!) and there is a kind of Hindu *Americanness* about me that feels more similar to their peers than to their parents. (Most Hindu American kids' parents immigrated after 2000.)

The girls are shocked to hear that I've never been to In-N-Out before. A flurry of grilled, cheesy, fried, and creamy goodies fuels some very animated adolescent gossip and Instagram scrolling. And then we're bursting out of the air-conditioned oasis into the hot, dry summer evening through the parking lot to the car. My sundress has wilted from the day's sweat. Walking beside me, hanging close, is one of my new car friends. She is in skinny jeans, an oversized T-shirt, baggy sweatshirt loosely hanging off her shoulders, and a baseball cap covering her beautiful, enormous brown eyes. Her bangs peek out from underneath the brim. Her smile is magnetic.

Her name is Yagnee[8] and she is the daughter of Milind Makwana, a community leader I had heard much about and was on my list of potential interviewees.

Sadly, a couple of weeks before I arrived in California, Milind suddenly passed away from a heart attack at just 44 years old. He was a passionate advocate and deeply beloved. A shocked community rallied around his wife and young children, including his best friend, Akshay. This made it even more remarkable that they still wanted to participate in my study. It was humbling to hear about Milind throughout my time in the Bay, about how he impacted so many lives.

Milind Makwana

Milind was instrumental in spreading the word about Hindu values that he believed stimulated a democratic way of thinking and an acceptance of different perspectives.

AI and Faith's Board Chair David Brenner interviewed Milind Makwana as their new Advisor for AI product development and Faith Employee Resource Groups (ERGs). He asks Milind how his Hindu faith influences how he engages in his work and leadership.

"Hindus believe that each *aatma* (loosely translated to soul) is potentially divine which enables us to see everyone equal," said Milind. "Hindus follow the four goals of life (*Purusharthas*) namely: *Dharma* (righteousness), *Artha* (material wealth), *Kama* (desire) and *Moksha* (liberation). Empathy and compassion together are one of the core values of Hindu, and also one of the important skills required in today's corporate world. Being Hindu stimulates a democratic way of thinking, accepting various viewpoints as seen from different perspectives. One cannot overestimate the importance of these values in today's world."

It is striking how often he is described as a *sevak* (someone dedicated to selfless service). Milind's volunteer work was not the low-hanging fruit type. He traveled to India in 2015 to volunteer in Tamil Nadu after the floods. He was at the forefront of relief efforts after the 2020 California wildfires. The list goes on. Milind also wrote an illustrated children's book, *A Day in the Life of a Hindu Kid: Kid's Hindu Prayer, Rhyming and Activity Book*, to introduce young Hindu Americans to *mantras* (Sanskrit prayers).

Most powerfully, I read his own words:

> I immigrated to the United States with the hope
> of building a better life for my family. My father,
> like his father before him, spent much of his early

life as a daily wage earner doing carpentry work and other odd jobs. Barely making ends meet, he, my mother, my younger brother and sister, and I lived in Mumbai's infamous chawls—crowded, low-quality tenements—where we rented a small, cramped room from a relative.

Though it would be easy to assume the area was probably filled with families from castes like ours, the truth was we were surrounded by people of all linguistic, social, and occupational backgrounds, be they teachers, small business owners, or other daily wage workers. We all lived harmoniously, helping one another when needed, bemoaning the difficulties of barely making ends meet, and celebrating festivals and special occasions together. Not once did we experience any sort of ostracization based on our caste.

Wanting to give his family a better life with better opportunities, my father eventually earned a two-year diploma in interior design and moved our family of five out of the chawls into a 400-square-foot apartment in Mumbai. We were on our way to a solid, lower middle-class life.

Our neighbors included a priest and a Vedic astrologer. While both were members of what some would deem India's "upper" or "dominant" castes, we were all in the same socio-economic boat. We didn't think of them as superior, nor did they think of us as inferior. We too lived harmoniously, helping one another when needed, lamenting the struggles of upward mobility, and celebrating festivals and special occasions together.

Despite my father working multiple jobs tirelessly, he also found time to give back to not only our community but beyond it. He actively volunteered with a formal association that was established by members of our caste community. The association gave us a space to come together and celebrate the traditions that were unique to our community— the worship of Khodiyar Mata, for instance.

Our legends and traditions passed down orally for generations, meant that every full moon day was to be honored as a day of rest from work to be spent in worship and gratitude to our clan goddess. On the goddess's appearance day, we distributed books and other school supplies to children studying at a school for Harijan children (children from other marginalized communities) across the Khodyiar Mata temple or fed the priests who helped nourish and sustain our community members' worldly and spiritual needs. The association provided assistance to anyone in need, regardless of whether they were within our caste community.

Purvi Makwana[9] describes her husband's clear conviction that Dalits and Bahujans were part of the broader Hindu community. "He was passionate about justice for underprivileged communities and, at the same time, wanted mutual trust and harmony among all communities ... All his life, he stood for

Dharma," she said. "I urge the community to support and take forward Milind's dream of justice, harmony, and Dharma."[10]

As I read about him, I felt in my gut how wonderful it would have been to meet Milind Makwana, to hear his stories directly. His heart and his purpose still appear vibrant and continuous to me through the people that love him like his daughter, Yagnee—his legacy.

As we all walk back to the car, Yagnee and I talk about things that press on the mind of a 15-year-old girl as we pile back into the car with her cousin from Los Angeles, and Akshay's two daughters, one of whom is Yagnee's best friend. When we arrive back at Akshay's house, Yagnee pulls me aside. "I want you to interview me," she said.

I haven't talked too much about my research with the girls during our little adventure. In fact, I have barely mentioned it. And I have certainly not broached the topic of interviewing any of them, especially since Akshay discreetly informed me who Yagnee was before we left. My priority is honoring her process and supporting her in whatever way I can.

But clearly, Yagnee has something she wants to say. Consent forms are signed. We find a quiet-ish spot in Akshay's bustling house and she shares her story. Even as she is gentle in affect, there is a clarity and resolve shining through her. She refuses to use a pseudonym. She says,

"I want people to know who I am. That I said this."

Yagnee's mother, Purvi, later tells me that Yagnee means "one who is the recipient of all the offerings into the *Yagna* (divine fire)."

Yagnee Makwana

As we settle in the room for the interview, the door bursts open. Yagnee's younger brother launches inside, frantic. He needs confirmation with his own eyes that she is there. He has been playing with Akshay's son throughout the day, but he makes sure that his big sister is always in view. While he giggles and squeals in that sweet 10-year-old way, every so often his face falls as you see him remembering what has happened. It's only been 17 days since his father passed away. My heart aches for him.

The siblings exchange glances. She soothes him, assuring him she is still in the house and instructs him to continue playing with his friend. Her voice is layered with compassion and maturity. Reassured, he runs back outside. When she turns back to me, she smiles. It is not a superficial smile. This is a kind human being.

There is a depth in Yagnee's presence that is unusual for someone her age. Perhaps it is the grace and strength that can emerge when a young person loses a parent too soon. Or maybe this is how she has always been, how she chooses to navigate her fresh grief. And, still, she is also a regular teenager. We start off by talking about her love of reading, cooking, baking, and, of course, Taylor Swift. She tells me she's really passionate about being empathetic and kind, a quality that I have seen her embody in her interactions. She connects this kindness back to the Hindu values her parents have instilled in her, of karma and Dharma.

(I notice Yagnee switching between present and past tense when she's talking about her father, but not as a painful correction. It feels more like a natural expression of his memory and his uninterrupted presence.)

We talk about what it's like growing up with immigrant parents, a conversation that began in the car with everyone else. She shares that it's been quite easy, as her parents are open-minded, encouraging her to appreciate the good things about all countries. I relate to this because it is how I was raised; that it was possible to love and appreciate two very different places—India and the U.S.—at the same time. And then she says something that strikes me as quite perceptive—that while she loves a lot of things about India, she wouldn't want to live there but not for the reasons you might think. "I don't really like the idea of being around a ton of people who look exactly like me and have the same culture as me. I really like the diversity here."

Yagnee is energized by the landscape of immigrant experiences and expressions in the U.S. As a scholar of education and immigration, this lights me up! She shares that, in fact, it was a Hungarian immigrant, and also one of her best friends, who was one of the first people at school to pronounce her name correctly. We talk about what it's like to have your name mispronounced by so many people at school that it seems futile to try and change it. But something clicked for Yagnee the previous year, her freshman year in high school.

"This year I started correcting people, and the more people I corrected, the more people started correcting other people for me," she said. "And I felt like that validated me a lot. I felt like, oh, people care."

The deeper lessons in this aren't lost on me. That our inner monologue about what is possible isn't necessarily reality. That the people around us may be open to learning and changing, especially if that change reflects kindness and greater mutual respect. And that this kind of positive change can be contagious and can only happen if we try. Yagnee shares that this kind of learning is how her parents think of school. As she shares, it is clear to me that the kindness Yagnee's parents have instilled in her is not about social niceness. It is a principled kindness that is committed to self-knowledge, responsibility, respect, and community. It is also clear that their family's values are an expression of being Hindu in the world.

Yagnee learned about Hinduism in *shakha*, which literally translates to branch. Shakha refers to the local chapters that form a larger network called the Hindu Swayamsevak Sangh (HSS). Each Shakha serves as a community hub for diaspora Hindu families who are interested in joining. (Not all Hindu Americans are connected to a Shakha; there are other communities of Hindu Americans.) Shakhas conduct weekly gatherings, providing lessons on Hinduism and community building exercises. (It is not something I grew up with or even knew about until a few years ago! I have since been learning just how significant a role it plays in supporting the Hindu heritage education of countless Hindu American children.) The larger national network creates a feeling of cohesion for a religious community that is tiny and dispersed across a large nation. There are HSS's around the world.

Yagnee's parents didn't grow up attending Shakha in India (there is an India-based version), but when they moved to the

U.S., they began appreciating its value, even before Yagnee was born. Shakha now means the world to her.

"It has given me my family," Yagnee said. "I love my biological family, of course, but my Shakha family—the bond is something no one can ever break. And when my dad passed, they were all there for me last week. As soon as it was late at night, they all drove over. My house wasn't silent at all. Everyone was there. Everyone was helping me out. Shakha people will always be there for me. That's something I know for sure. And my best friend. I've met most of my best friends through Shakha. It's taught me all my values, too. Kindness. Treat everyone like they're your family."

I don't know what it's like to grow up being part of such a large network of Hindu Americans, but I can see the profound impact it's had on this young woman's life, on her connection with being Hindu. She's not sure if she believes in God. I'm just kind of iffy about it," she says, which I can completely understand given what is happening in her life. But she aligns with the philosophical aspect of Hinduism. This is the beauty of being Hindu, a foundational beauty and acceptance that doesn't get picked up on surveys of religiosity. You can be unsure about the existence of God and still be Hindu, still be connected to the principles of Hinduism.

Yagnee believes that the most important Hindu principle is acceptance. (This is a common theme I hear from Hindu Americans of all generations and ages.) It isn't lost on her that while other religions in America may be values driven, they also believe that people will go to hell if they don't believe in their religion. This is something I have long noticed and wondered about as Hindu in America. Ironically, it often feels like conversations about diversity are dependent on sameness rather than pluralism. Yagnee has noticed this, too. She also observes that for Hindus, our identities are not tied to markers like race and gender but to our values of acceptance, openness, and kindness and how these beliefs impact our actions in the world. Ironically, she notes, there are a lot of misconceptions out there that Hinduism and Hindus are inherently misogynistic and homophobic. This is part of the Hindu American experience—speaking within a context of stereotypes and misconceptions that are deeply embedded in the public imagination. Yagnee believes that being Hindu American means first accepting who you are in this society and then standing up for who you are.

"People will misunderstand you," she said. "They will judge you. They will think bad things, and you should stand up and prove those things wrong."

I notice the tone of acceptance with which she articulates this. There is not a resignation or frustration in her voice. There isn't a quiver of injustice that Hindus are uniquely oppressed in American society. It is simply a matter of fact. There will always be people who misunderstand you and to navigate this you must first know yourself, and from that place of self-knowledge, you stand up and prove them wrong. This resonates deeply for me. As I said earlier, there is an unusual depth of wisdom and clarity in this unassuming young woman.

Yagnee has always felt confident in being Hindu, unlike some of her classmates. When I ask her about her experiences being Hindu in school, she tells me that she hasn't experienced much racism or bigotry from white students. In fact, she's found them to be quite kind and accepting. On the other hand, she has felt other Hindu students projecting their shame and rejection of their Hinduness onto her.

This doesn't surprise me. I have seen other Hindu Americans operate with the assumption that to be accepted as American they must outwardly (and, perhaps, inwardly) reject Hinduism. This assumption isn't a fixed reality, but these inner and outer dialogues can feel complicated and immutable. I find it can be generative to surface and loosen assumptions by modeling that sometimes it's not complicated at all. It's why I sometimes choose to wear a sari and/or a bindi when I am speaking "as an American." I defended my doctoral dissertation in a bindi and a sari. I once wore a blue blouse and a red bindi to speak at a congressional hearing about students' experiences with Hinduphobia. I am an American who sometimes wears a bindi because I'm Hindu.

Yagnee wanted to do something similar. She thought it was cute that her friend was wearing a bindi to school, so she showed up the next day wearing one.

"I felt so pretty that day," she said. "And I was waiting for my first period to start, and this (Hindu American) girl tells me to take it off. So I haven't worn a bindi since then to school. It's always the Indians, the Indian Hindus. It's never going to be anyone else. It's always the people who do the same things as you. I feel like they're ashamed of their culture. They're projecting that insecurity on other people. I feel like they think, 'I need to fit in. I need to be like everyone else. So to fit in as an American kid in school, I can't show that I'm Hindu.'"

Bindi

A bindi is a sacred mark, often a red dot, worn by Hindu girls and women on the forehead between the eyebrows. It symbolizes spiritual insight, the inner eye, and one's connection to the Divine. While many people today use a small adhesive sticker bindi in a variety of shapes and colors, the traditional bindi is made of *kumkum*, a fine, deep red powder prepared from turmeric and lime and associated with auspiciousness and the presence of the sacred. There are many forms of this practice across Hindu communities: the bindi (or *pottu*, in some languages) is associated with women; the *tilak*, *namam*, or *chandan* may be worn by men. Styles vary in color, shape, region, and philosophical variations. Though they look different, they all convey a shared understanding that the Divine resides within each person. For many in India, wearing these marks is simply an everyday practice. For those of us who grew up outside of India, these marks can symbolize how we navigate belonging between our home and public lives.

What is it that is happening in American schools that might make some Hindu Americans feel a need to not only hide their Hinduness but to be ashamed of Hindu expression? What was happening in Yagnee's school? Well, to begin with, they didn't talk about Hinduism that much. And when they did, it was in sixth grade, in a video about ancient Indian civilization.

The video was fixated on the idea that caste hierarchy and caste oppression were foundational to Hinduism. Little else was shared about Hinduism. Afterward, her classmates' main takeaway was not about the beauty of Hindu philosophy or civilization, but that Hinduism was cruel and oppressive.

I could feel Yagnee's shock in that moment acutely. I wonder if you can. Imagine feeling so connected to the beauty of your ancestral tradition, so much depth of wisdom, so much openness and acceptance. Imagine growing up as a part of a community tied to that tradition, down to the roots. Imagine that this shapes your entire stance of operating from radical kindness in the world. And then pretend that your school ignores Hinduism for your entire childhood and, all of a sudden, your sixth-grade teacher uses a video to teach your classmates that the entire tradition—the culture, the philosophy, the knowledge, the civilization—is rooted in oppression. As if its very purpose is to harm. And then imagine watching your classmates—including the most popular girl in class—internalize this opinion about your people and express disgust about your religion. It is not a surprise that the other Hindu girl told Yagnee to take off her bindi. She had been taught to be ashamed of being Hindu by her school. What power did a sixth grader have against this system of education? Who would be considered the authoritative voice?

Much of the time, children feel they have to protect their immigrant parents from the terrible ways their heritage is represented in school. But that's not what our Yagnee did. She went straight home and told her parents she needed to do something about this. This was such an important choice she made. Her father's response was perfect. (Remember, Milind

Makwana came from what is considered a lower-caste community in India and was a passionate activist and community leader about issues related to misrepresentations of caste in the U.S. This wasn't his first rodeo!) He clarified to his daughter that caste was not about a pyramid of hierarchy.

"He told me to clear up that it wasn't a system where one caste is on top and one caste is at the bottom," she said. "It was (about) different structures of society and different jobs you have, basically. And (this structure) kept society together. And one thing he told me was, imagine a man or a *deva* (deity). So the head would be Brahmin (a higher caste) and then feet would be Shudras (a lower caste). But it's not top to bottom. Imagine the man laying down on a bed. They're all equal, but the feet work really hard. So they are Shudras.

Equipped with this new metaphor of a man in repose, Yagnee went back to school and told her teacher about how the video had gotten it all wrong. She remembers her teacher being kind and very receptive to this information. This is so important and so common. It's important to remember that we cannot know each other perfectly. To know each other imperfectly is not a failure or a breakdown but an opportunity to create greater understanding. And we do that by taking a risk and sharing effectively and listening humbly. We are well served to believe in a prevailing attitude of openness and kindness. In fact, when it came time to do a standard flashcard exercise about Hinduism, the teacher incorporated the new information Yagnee had shared and adapted the exercise for the whole class. This made Yagnee feel that her teacher really cared.

This experience created such a strong impression on Yagnee that I can feel its impact as she is sharing with me. She believes in calling people in, rather than assuming that her first option is to call them out. In fact, this is something she learned a couple of years earlier, when she testified before the California Board of Education. When I ask her why she decided to testify, she giggles and tells me she thought it would be cool to talk in front of people who are part of the legal system. And also because she'd be on TV! (She was in fourth grade at the time.) On the road to Sacramento, her father gave her evidence about misrepresentations of Hinduism in their textbooks. Even as an eight-year-old, it was clear to her that these were unfair representations.

"So I wrote my speech and I put all my effort into it," she said. "And then when I was about to testify, I was thinking, this is something that I really hope makes an impact because what's happening is wrong and I want it to change."

I ask Yagnee if her parents scripted her speech. I tell her that some vocal scholars and journalists have been saying for years that the Hindu kids who testified in California were fed speeches and forced to testify. Yagnee snickers. "My dad's the one who was always involved in everything, and he told me to do it for my heart. And if it wasn't for my heart, then I shouldn't do it for anyone else." This has been the underlying pulse throughout our hour-long conversation. Yagnee has been raised as a Hindu, which means being deeply connected through her heart to a sense of being kind and doing the right thing in and for the world. There is not a shred of indoctrination or dogma in what she has described explicitly or conveyed implicitly.

This manifests in the moments when she calls people in to correct misconceptions about Hinduism and Hindus. Yagnee doesn't remember what she said in her speech before the board of education. But she *does* remember that her parents sent the video of her testimony to her fourth-grade teacher. Her teacher brought her to the front of the classroom and played the video for the whole class.

She said, "I remember, I was leaning against the whiteboards, and everyone was watching attentively, watching my speech. And then when it ended, they all started applauding for me. And then they said, play it again. Play it again. And my teacher literally played it again, and they applauded even more! I felt like, oh my God, they care about me. I felt really validated."

I imagine what that must have been like for a 10-year-old. She followed her heart and chose to testify before a state panel of legislators. She wrote and delivered her own speech. Her classmates watched a video of her speech afterward while she stood in front of the classroom *watching them watch her*. (Think of what that must have been like!) And then they applauded and asked to watch it again! What did that do for her sense of possibility? I think about how Yagnee's parents taught her the impact of speaking out but also about how her parents took a risk sending that video to her teacher. And how her teacher not only taught the entire class the importance of civic participation, but how people their age actively participate in American democracy! I can hear those kiddos clapping for Yagnee—the joy they must have felt in watching one of their peers stand bravely in front of a panel of bureaucrats and speak from her heart about her tradition and ancestral land. Yagnee tells me that afterward that her friends wanted to understand more about why she went to speak out and how open they were to really understand what she had to say.

I think about this vibrant and hopeful reality of young Americans and how disconnected it is from the bogeyman imagery painted by scholars and journalists who have never bothered to ask Yagnee and her peers about their experiences and motivations.

A Condensed Origin Story of Early American Public Education and National Identity

It is fascinating to observe the different ways people talk about the purpose of a K-12 education. Whether it is in a classroom of emergent teachers, immigrant communities, parent groups, public servants, your everyday online provocateur with a hot take, or a quippy meme making the rounds, it becomes fairly obvious that we're not always talking about the same thing even though we all call it school. Some of the popular ideas that we see circulating today about the purpose of school include:

School should give young people the practical skills they need for adult life such as how to file taxes, fiscal responsibility, and professional skills. They're never going to use the Pythagorean theorem.

Schools should teach our children foundational knowledge in all the subject areas beginning with reading and writing.

Schools should prepare our young people to be tomorrow's leaders and thinkers. They should teach our children how to think, not what to think.

Schools are community institutions. They not only educate our children, they are havens that provide safety, shelter, and food for vulnerable children who are not getting it elsewhere.

Schools shouldn't provide free meals. This creates dependency and lets families off the hook.

Schools should not be teaching morality. That is up to parents.

Schools produce future generations of upstanding citizens in our democracy.

Schools and education should not be politicized. It should not be hijacked by political agendas. A good education is neutral.

Schools and education are inherently political. What we decide is worth knowing is inherently informed by power. Pretending it is neutral camouflages the power dynamics.

Schools are the key to uplifting society. They are our hope.

Schools have to deal with all of the problems and failings of society. That isn't fair or realistic.

I could keep going, but you get the picture. People not only believe very different things about the purpose of school, often those ideas are in direct contradiction to each other. This is not as simple as disagreement. People are bringing layers of assumptions into the conversation about school. Sometimes, especially in the case of immigrants, they are bringing histories of educational policy, practices, and attitudes from very different contexts. For instance, if you were educated in a post-colonial nation like India, it is highly likely that the pedagogical model (practice of teaching) you experienced centered on rote learning, versus original thinking. This is because the educational system was inherited from the colonizer who designed schools to teach obedience. This system takes up the banking model of education, where the student is seen as an empty vessel into which the teacher, who holds the information, pours knowledge. (This is not to say that India does not produce original thinkers. Of course not! However, the *concept* of school, especially primary and secondary education, is influenced by these factors.) So the conversation about the purpose of school is not just about the purpose of school. It reveals assumptions, experiences, and histories about how school happens, how it ought to happen, and why it should happen.

Unfortunately, most of the time, people do not surface or interrogate or question any of this. They may not even be aware of them. Most of the time, people are just talking across each other, thinking they are having the same conversation when that isn't actually the case.

In other words, "the purpose of school" conversation … is complicated.

It might surprise you to learn that the secondary public school system that we know today emerged during the Industrial Revolution, when it became important to certain interests to produce a steady work force that was disciplined and semi-skilled. David Tyack and Larry Cuban observe how secondary education expanded during the late 19th and early 20th century as a direct result of industrial demands for disciplined laborers.[11] The concept of mandatory education emerged at the same time, as a result of the influence of industrialists and educational reformers.

In their 1976 analysis of the system of American schooling in the context of our economic system, Samuel Bowles and Herbert Gintis[12] document how the National Association of Manufacturers (NAM) conducted a decades-long campaign to establish compulsory schooling to ensure a continuous workforce supply. This coincided with the efforts of Progressive Era educational administrators, such as school superintendents, state boards, and other bureaucrats, to create centralized systems of education with standardized curriculum.[13] Their motivations may have been distinct—industrialists pursuing their interests and educational bureaucrats seeking public service through systemization—but the confluence of these efforts resulted in public education as we know it today.

For schools to produce a workforce, industrialists were invested in shifting *what* was taught in schools. From the late 1890s until World War I, virtually every national NAM conference passed resolutions advocating vocational education.[14] It was at this time that urban high schools started including vocational tracks as a part of schooling, competing with and replacing the older apprenticeship model that had been situated for generations in guilds and families.[15]

The Industrial Revolution not only influenced the purpose and requirement of schooling, it played a role in *how* schooling happened. Frederick Taylor's scientific management model, known as Taylorism, heavily influenced the factory-like model of school organization that focused on efficiency and outputs from standardized procedures to hierarchical administration.[16]

This contributes to why many people, today, conflate formal secondary education (and not apprenticeships)[17] with job readiness.[18]

It is important to note, in this very brief survey of American educational history, that there were contemporary educators who vigorously disagreed with these shifts in schooling for American children, including influential educator John Dewey and other educational scholars and leaders who viewed factory efficiency and standardization as obstacles to reflective, autonomous inquiry and discovery.

> The ideal aim of education is creation of
> power of self-control. It is not the process
> of acquiring habits imposed from without,
> but of the formation of habits freely and
> intelligently directed to ends.
>
> – John Dewey[19]

Educational scholars describe how this link between schools and industry led to intelligence testing designed to determine students' ability to participate in the workforce[20] and the arrival of special education categories that reinforced existing social prejudices.[21] We will discuss shifts and discourses in American education more in Chapters Three and Four.

Take a moment now to go back to those statements about the purpose of school from the beginning of this chapter and see if you can trace some of their origin stories in the history we just covered.

So what came before this movement to standardized, mandatory public education, the expansion of secondary education, and their link with industry? Let's go back in time to the 19th century, right after American independence. Before we arrived at the unified contemporary public school system, there were various forms of primary and secondary schools in the newly formed United States. School didn't signify one thing in the early days of the republic. Churches ran schools in their communities that taught not only Bible studies but literacy and numeracy; some of these were established before independence.[22] Informal home schools dotted the landscape, especially since many girls didn't have access or the means to attend formal school, especially those from poor, rural families. Quaker communities had their own schools and approaches to teaching that focused on egalitarianism. Various immigrant and ethnic communities ran schools where the language of instruction might be German, Yiddish, or Polish. There were Irish Catholic parochial schools and tribal schools on Native American reservations (we'll expand on that in Chapter Three). Then there were the private schools for the elite[23] where the young men of high society, who would later become the leaders in government and industry, would study fine art and literature.[24] After emancipation, formerly enslaved people invested their resources and opened up schools for their children,[25] recognizing the significant role literacy would play in their children's future participation as citizens.

The repertoire of and access to various forms of schools reflected the incredible range of American society, across socioeconomics, religion, ethnicity, language, political power, pedagogical approaches, and purpose. It was in the midst of this diversity and disparity in the 1830s, that Horace Mann presented his idea of the *common* school.[26] Mann envisioned school as an incubator of citizenship and society-building in a new and novel democracy that believed "all men are created equal."

> Education then, beyond all other devices of
> human origin, is the great equalizer of the
> conditions of men, the balance-wheel of the
> social machinery.
>
> – Horace Mann, *Annual Reports on Education*

Thus arrived a new idea of the purpose of school in the United States—public education as a mechanism to create social harmony in a society plagued by class disparity. This idea of education as an equalizer, as a way to balance out the "social machinery," was the first iteration of the American school that aspired not only to welcome students from different economic backgrounds to learn the subjects together but, at least in theory, to function harmoniously within the walls of the school. It is important to note that Mann neither implicitly nor explicitly sought to remedy or challenge inequity through instruction; his vision was to mitigate its effects through the school's civic education and moral community. Mann's "inclusive" design was still quite exclusive in practice; schools were segregated by race, curricula was gendered, and Indigenous and disabled children were excluded. However, it represented a shift toward a shared public education system that served the general population.

1837 marked the beginning of the Common School Era with the establishment of the Massachusetts Board of Education and Horace Mann as its first secretary.[27] Public schools existed in Boston as early as the 1600s, but Mann's Common School represented a novel and systematic push for free, non-sectarian education that served children of all classes. This state-sponsored system envisioned public education as the site of production of the American citizen. "Common Schooling was, above all, a political project: a strategy for creating a unified citizenry through the shared experience of public education."[28]

K-12 education was no longer just a somewhat disjointed array of communities' disparate educational goals and ideas. It now included—at least in theory—the possibility of realizing a shared vision, across class, of the *character of the American citizen through education*. Curriculum included attention on civics and ethics,[29] courses to help shape the ideal American. This was explicitly tied to Enlightenment values like reason, virtue, and civic participation. Schools were given the mandate to instill American children with good Enlightenment habits, such as industry, punctuality, and morality.[30]

"Education came to be regarded as the essential safeguard of republican government, the principal means of developing the reason and virtue upon which the republic depended."[31]

This was not just an introspective exercise—American democracy was developed on a global stage. American citizenry was, therefore, about the United States in contrast to the world, reflecting broader global dynamics and power structures, and the need for the new American democracy and its citizens to represent something *different*.

"Schools were to be the proving ground of democracy, not only for internal harmony but also as a demonstration to the world that a republic could educate all its children and survive."[32]

Thus, according to educational historian Lawrence Cremin, American public education, beginning with the Common School Era, evolved into more than a national project of citizen-building.

It became a global symbol—a beacon—of the ideals of American democracy,[33] and eventually, a cultural export.

The history of American public education is filled with aspirations that school could be the great equalizer, that citizenship could be learned and lived, and that communities could grow stronger through shared participation in civic life. For many Americans, civic commitments are deeply spiritual. The next story offers a glimpse into a family whose public service, persistence, and belief in education's power are inseparable from its Hindu values, which see the divine in all beings and call for *seva* (service) as a form of worship.

Pammi's Home: Dharma and Community

The first thing you notice about Pammi's home is how it seems designed to welcome people. The spacious, sunlit great room with elegant touches feels less like a display of taste and more like an invitation to melt into their vibrant chatter, as if you had always been a part of the conversation. The light falls softly across furniture arranged to encourage conversation, and everywhere there are signs of hospitality: extra chairs in the corner, serving dishes stacked within easy reach, the faint aroma of spices lingering from a recent meal. This is a house ready for family, for friends, for community. In Pammi's family, the ideals of American democracy—service, dignity, equality, responsibility—are not philosophical abstractions. It is part of a daily practice braided with Hindu principles that honors the divinity in all beings.

Pammi is the heart of this home. Her voice is like a sweet song, warm and lilting, a melody that always seems on the verge of laughter. She speaks with a smile, and when she talks about her family, that smile glows brighter still. They are, by every measure, close—bound together by affection, respect, and a shared sense of purpose. Service, for them, is not an occasional act. It is the heartbeat of their life together, inseparable from their Hindu faith.

Pammi's journey to this life began in India where she earned her law degree. After immigrating to the U.S., she found ways to use her skills in service to others. She volunteered at a shelter for women who had survived domestic violence and at an immigration clinic, conducting intake interviews. Later, when her two children were in fourth and first grade, she decided to pursue a paralegal certification at the local community center.

It was a natural continuation of her education, but after completing the program, she couldn't find a job in the field. Instead, she poured her time into her children's school. Through the PTA, she helped organize events, meeting other parents she describes as very accepting.

"My children were not invited to a lot of birthday parties," she remembers. "They thought that probably they wouldn't fit in or I don't know why, but it didn't matter. But the parents were all very welcoming and very nice. And whenever we had children here, or even the parents, they were very respectful about leaving their shoes outside, asking about our culture and all of that. And they would ask us about our Gods and all of that. So yeah, they're still my friends. I still see them and meet them often."

Those friendships lasted, as did Pammi's connection to her children's school community. Eventually, she found herself back in the classroom—this time as a teacher.

"I work with adults 17 and a half and older." she said. "So this year my oldest graduate was a 68-year-old man from Mexico. So most of the students are from the marginalized population; they are immigrants. Some of them are professionals back in their country, but because of the situation there they can't go back, get their certificates, diplomas, or whatever. So this kind of gives me perspective in life, to see how fortunate I am. So I have students who work two jobs, then come and attend my class."

Pammi hadn't set out to become a teacher. She was looking for a part-time job that fit her children's school schedule, so she could still drop them off and pick them up. She started as an instructional aide, working for about a year and a half before earning her teaching credentials from the University of California, Berkeley Extension. Her students came with a range of motivations.

"Some of them are not really checked in; they're only there because it's required by the county or school district," she said. "But for most of them, it's kind of a life-changing thing. For some of them, it's a personal goal. For a lot of them, it's getting the GED. It gives them a better job, better life, which they would've never done otherwise. And they're very fortunate to be in this country. And this is the last chance for these students before they go to the real world. It's the last stop."

She glows when she talks about them. Her work is not without its risks, something her mother back in India often reminds her of.

"My mom's very scared because especially with all the gun violence going on," she said. "She's like, some of your students have mental health issues. She's like, 'Oh, you need to be careful. This is what you want to do.' But of course, when I tell her stories about the way some of them come back, even after years, to thank me, she's like, 'Oh yeah, it's a good thing that you're doing good karma.'"

Her Hinduism weaves naturally into her teaching life.

"My director is also a Hindu, and I educate my students about Hinduism," she said. "On Diwali, I take a write-up on what Diwali is, leave it in my staff lounge with some sweets. Same thing in my classroom. My students are kind of oblivious to a lot of things. They are caught up in their own everyday life. Bringing food to the table is a big deal for most of them. So I never get questions about a lot of things that we practice or how a Hindu life is. But my colleagues, like I told you, they do ask about caste. One of my colleagues asked me, are you the upper caste? Is that why you're in this country? So are people still being oppressed? And are there a lot of beggars in India? Are you scared to take your kids there because it's not clean and there's no running water? Things like that. Basically, what the textbook or what a lot of what they read, that's the kind of image they have."

Pammi's approach to these questions is as steady and warm as she is in every other part of her life. She answers them honestly; with the same care she gives her students. Her children have grown up in this atmosphere—of service, faith, and conversation, and each reflects it in their own way.

Her daughter Meghana, now in college, finds echoes of her Hindu upbringing in the ideals she has learned about in American history. "I think a lot of the American values and the American history really resonates with the Hindu values that I was taught. For example, some of the abolitionist movements were inspired by Hinduism, meaning specifically about how every person has a soul divinity and they should all be respected and treated the same, treated equally, which is a very common Hindu value. So yeah, lots of things in that way. And even with the way that I politically am, I think a lot of it comes back to my Hindu values. I truly believe in climate change and protecting the environment, and I do as much as I can at home to help with that but also to make sure to vote in that way politically."

Pammi's husband, Ram, shares this commitment to community and has a grounded perspective on what it takes to participate in American democracy.

"This country, while it has been a democracy for 200-odd years, it still has got a long way for it to make to a democracy that people can all speak their voice and actually be heard, and which, by firsthand experience, I can tell unless you're firm enough, nobody will listen to you," Ram said "Like I said, the first two hearings, the moderator had the summary written even before we spoke. So she didn't hear us. But because we didn't give up. We went again, we went again, and then they finally listened to us. We give it our all. So that's one thing. This country is that way. I recognize that now. Exactly what it was in the beginning, right? It's not perfect. It took me some time to figure out that it's not perfect. It's all this beautiful thing. I say it's not perfect. And at the same time, I would tell everybody that you can make a difference. There is hope. It's not, I don't want to admit that everything's gloom and doom. No, you can engage as an individual, as a community. You can make a difference."

Ram's belief in persistence echoes his roots. In his coastal Karnataka village, where his family can trace its lineage back 800 years, he learned what it means to be woven into the fabric of a place. Here in the U.S., he has built similar kinds of connections—helping neighbors, offering his skills to anyone in need, quietly strengthening the bonds of the local community.

Their son Anirudh, now in medical school, frames his Hinduism in expansive terms.

"For me being a Hindu is to understand that everything in the world is connected. It's not only everyone, everything that is the nature, living things, non-living things, animals, everything is connected. Being Hindus mean 'a belief that there is divinity within everything.' Everyone, everything. And our job is to serve. That service to humankind is service to God. So I think serving the community, serving each other, I think that's serving God."

> I think in a time where there are sort of social
> forces or certain folks that make it seem like
> you can't be one or the other, I think it's really
> clear that we're here, we're American, and
> we're Hindu, and we're here to do our karma
> and our Dharma in this country.
>
> – Anirudh

CHAPTER TWO

Kill the Hindu, Save the American

A great general has said that the only good
Indian is a dead one, and that high sanction
of his destruction has been an enormous
factor in promoting Indian massacres. In a
sense, I agree with the sentiment, but only
in this: that all the Indian there is in the race
should be dead. Kill the Indian in him, and
save the man.

– Captain Richard Henry Pratt, the (1892)
National Conference of Charities and Correction,
in Denver, Colorado.[34]

If you've heard of the phrase "Kill the Indian, save the man,"
this is where it originates.

What is remarkable, when you read the entirety of Pratt's
speech, is that although he is overtly calling for cultural genocide, it doesn't seem like *he* believes he harbors any animosity

towards Native Americans. Quite the opposite—he believes it is his responsibility to save them. This is the white man's burden that Rudyard Kipling,[35] born in British India, would write about a few years later.[36]

The white man's burden was an imperialist belief that Western powers had a *moral* obligation to civilize non-Western people. Remember that morality was an essential habit of the upstanding, enlightened American citizen.

Pratt shows incredible remorse for the suffering Native Americans endured, not only because of war with the settlers and the new American government, but through treaties with the U.S. government that kept them on reservations, "held apart from all association with the best of our civilization." Pratt also criticizes how white men have benefited financially from these treaties, at the expense of the fiscal stability and growth of Native Americans. For 1892, that's pretty progressive thinking.

He even goes so far as to cite the Roman historian Tacitus saying, "The human mind is so constituted as to make us hate those whom we have wronged." Pratt goes on to talk about how the U.S. has oppressed Black people for too long and how we have finally progressed past the disturbing history of enslavement. In his description, he reveals a lot of assumptions about that progress. He says:

> Horrible as were the experiences of its introduction, and of slavery itself, there was concealed in them the greatest blessing that ever came to the Negro race—seven millions of blacks from cannibalism in darkest Africa to citizenship in free and enlightened America; not full, not complete

citizenship, but possible—probable—citizenship, and on the highway and near to it.

Pratt goes on to say that this "citizen-making" did not happen through formal education, as Black people were denied access to schools; it happened through "the influences of association." There is a lot to unpack throughout his entire speech, but a key thread here is that Pratt believed that while slavery was horrible, it eventually led to a positive outcome. Not only because slavery ended, but because the race of people who were enslaved were able to become enlightened, away from their previously unenlightened ("darkest") ways and probably move toward equal citizenship.

It's important to take a pause here and see that all these years later, while many of us might see what is troubling about Pratt's assumptions, we can also see that Pratt's vision mimics later language of inclusion while being rooted in domination and cultural erasure.

The word "unenlightened" is a direct reference to Enlightenment ideals, you'll remember from Chapter Two, which were held as the moral compass for nation building through American education. Pratt continues:

> However great this victory has been for us, we have not yet fully learned our lesson nor completed our work; nor will we have done so until there is throughout all of our communities the most unequivocal and complete acceptance of our own doctrines, both national and religious. Not until there shall be in every locality throughout

the nation a supremacy of the Bible principle of the brotherhood of man and the fatherhood of God, and full obedience to the doctrine of our Declaration that "we hold these truths to be self-evident, that all men are created free and equal, with certain inalienable rights," and of the clause in our Constitution which forbids that there shall be "any abridgment of the rights of citizens on account of race, color, or previous condition."

What did this have to do with Native Americans? Pratt explains that Native Americans did not have the same opportunity as Black people to become citizen-like because placing them on reservations denied them the very associations that might "improve" them. He criticized tribal schools for maintaining tribal education, rather than educating their students toward citizenship. Said Pratt: "We shall not succeed in Americanizing the Indian unless we take him in exactly the same way [as we do other assimilated groups]."

What did this mean in practice? The establishment of the Native American boarding school system began with The Carlisle Indian Industrial School founded in Carlisle, Pennsylvania, in 1879. The goal of these schools was to integrate Native American children into American society by first removing them from their tribal environments and then removing the "tribalness" inside of them. For Pratt, giving Native American children the opportunity to participate in American society by civilizing them away from their Native American culture was the decent and humanitarian thing to do to truly embrace Native Americans as a part of American citizenry.

Pratt may have believed in the nobility of his impulse, but the effect on the next five generations of Native Americans was devastating. One hundred thirteen years later, Ward Churchill published *Kill the Indian, Save the Man: The Genocidal Impact of American Indian Residential Schools.* Churchill's groundbreaking work is an unflinching examination of the effects of residential schools in the U.S. and Canada that lasted (at least) through 1990. Native American children were required to leave their home environments and attend these schools where they were compelled to communicate only in English and convert to Christianity. They were forbidden from using their Native languages, practicing their Native religions, or engaging in Native American cultural practices. The result was, as you might imagine, terrible. Skyrocketing mental health issues, maladaptive coping ... a complete fracturing of the Native American psyche. Ward identifies it as cultural genocide.

It is also important here to recognize Native American resistance to this state-sanctioned cultural genocide, and their contemporary efforts to reclaim their language and traditions both in collaboration with and independent of government institutions.

There is an important thread connecting this to the history and impact of American education on Hinduism. In fact, if you are a Hindu American, you may already be nodding. Before I pull this thread, though, let me be clear: I am in no way comparing the experiences of Hindu American children and families in the U.S. to the experiences (historical and contemporary) of Native American children and families.

Native American boarding schools operated from the assumption that the Heathen religion, culture, and society of Native

Americans were incompatible with American citizenship, which was seen as progressive and civilized and was modeled after the Protestant religion. To liberate Native American children from the inherently oppressive and regressive nature of their Indigenous ways, it had to be stripped away, both internally and externally. This is a thread that runs clearly through the large project of assimilation that was indistinguishable from the system of American public education that we discussed in Chapter One.

It's important to note that this is not based merely on race or ethnicity, but on their "heathen" way of looking at the world. In other words, it was about how Indigenous people perceived the world and not just how they were perceived *by* it. This is why it was possible to "save" them—by changing them on the *inside.*

It might surprise some of you to learn that Hinduism was another Heathen religion and culture and society that was seen as inherently oppressive and regressive and, therefore, incompatible with American democracy.

Long before Hindus set foot on American soil, before yoga studios popped up in strip malls and karma was a comeback on social media, Hinduism and Hindus were objects of fascination in the United States … including in American classrooms. This is surprising to many Americans, Hindus and non-Hindus alike. After all, why would American public education be interested in something on the other side of the world?

The Common School Era discussed in Chapter One marked the first attempt to organize an American public school that was central to the development of a new, coherent American education system. School textbooks played a central role in these new public schools, not only in converging curriculum but as a pedagogical tool (i.e., method of instruction).

As American education school scholar John Nietz explains:

> The textbook was the organizing principle in the schools of the early nineteenth century. It had to be, since the textbook was usually the only constant in a pupil's educational experience. Teachers might come and go, the child's family might move, his school attendance might be sporadic but the pupil always knew where he was educationally. He had completed his Primer, or he was half-way through Webster, or three-quarters into Murray. Pupils, and teachers, were able to use the textbooks this way to mark and record the pupil's progress because the textbooks dictated and controlled both the method of study and the method of instruction. Students memorized what was in the textbook, and teachers "heard" recitations.[37]

In a strange coincidence, it was at that time that missionary and early colonial reportage (through the East India Company) about India was filtering back to the United States. This was significant, as American democracy located its virtue and unique identity against a global context. Because of this, the study of geography was central in educating students about the differences between Americans and the rest of the world. Educational historian John Nietz described the four aims of geography textbooks[38] as: acquisition of knowledge; interest and entertainment; civic mindedness (both in terms of nationalism and a sense of the world); and cause and effect relationships. In other words, the study of geography gave American students a sense of how the world works.

As a part of this, geography textbooks also mapped human "hierarchies" by race, religion, and civilization.

Figure 2. Illustration from Samuel A. Mitchell's *A System of Modern Geography* (1840).

In his book *Heathen, Hindoo, Hindu: American Representations of India*, religious studies professor Michael J. Altman[39] describes how American textbooks shaped the contours of the ideal American citizen by using "Hindooism" as the dark space surrounding it. (I am indebted to Professor Altman for his deep research into this area. Until I read his book, I had no idea that there was such explicit curricula and imagery in 19th-century American textbooks.) Altman points specifically to Samuel Mitchell's 1840 book *A System of Modern Geography, Comprising a Description of the Present State of the World,* which was published and circulated as a standard geography text at the time.

"For schoolbook authors, Hindoo religion required violence," states Mitchell. "Violence served as more evidence for the degraded and pagan nature of Hindoo religion, further solidifying its place at the bottom of the religion hierarchy and further distancing Hindoos from the Christian child-reader. In addition to violence, schoolbook writers emphasized polytheistic and "idolatrous" themes in Hindoo religion—two themes that writers believed proved the falsity and moral degradation of Hindoo religion."[40]

Let's unpack this. We can see in this passage that "Hindoo" does not refer to the race of people, but to the image of a violent, immoral, and *false* religion that was conjured in the imagination of American children through schoolbooks. While India may have been referred to as "Hindoostan," it is not the nationality of the people that was under question: It was religion.

Foundational to the immorality and falseness of the Hindoo religion were polytheism and idol worship, which went against the very core of the three Western religions. This is important. Nineteenth-century American education had a system for understanding religious differences. In its simplest form, there were two categories: "false" and "true." The latter category included Christianity and, in a somewhat vague way, Judaism and Islam. Everything else was false. But these schoolbooks went a step further, creating an explicit way to tier the four main world religions—Christianity (including Protestant, Greek, and Catholic), Mahomedan (Islam), Jewish, and Pagan or Heathen.

Figure 3. Illustration of a Hindu devotee crawling across a rocky landscape (*Harper's Magazine*, 1867).[41]

Christians followed a real and true religion, centered on their belief in God, Jesus, and the entire Bible. Jews were a close runner up, with marks off for believing only in the Old Testament and God. The schoolbooks ranked Islam third, losing points as followers of a false prophet but also sharing a belief in God. The final category, Pagans and Heathens, believed entirely in false gods, worshipping the sun, moon, and animals. This was the worst of sins, and the three more "proper" religions coalesced around the fact that idolatry was the worst imaginable transgression.

Figure 4. Engraving from Samuel Mitchell's *A System of Modern Geography* (1867).[42]

The Heathen and Pagan religions included Native American and Hindu traditions. These were the furthest away from the top and furthest away from the good American child, not because the Hindoo child lived on the other side of the earth, but because the Hindoo child's superstitious beliefs and idolatry were bereft of the morality, reason, and civic participation of the Enlightened (Protestant) American child.

These ideas would last well past the 19th century. Historian David Kopf notes an expressed kinship with the Indian Muslim in contrast to an overt anti-Hindu bias in early 20th-century English literature set in India.[43] Kopf states:

> By Indianization, the British seem to mean Hinduization. It is the Hindus who have been exposed as the carriers of the deadly metaphysical disease known as life negation. Forster himself accepted Indian Muslims as being closer to the Western ideal. Nirad Chaudhuri believes that all the Hindus are presented in *Passage to India* 'either as perverted, clownish, or queer characters.' Even Dr. Godbole, Forster's chief Hindu character, and the novel's mouthpiece of Hinduism, is, in Chaudhuri's view, "not an exponent of Hinduism but a clown." On the other hand, the book's most rational Indian and chief Indian character, Aziz, is a Muslim.

Lawrence Brander, who has also written on Forster, made the following comparison about Hindus and Muslims in *Passage*: The first two parts of the novel are Muslim and Forster gets inside his Muslim characters with ease, for the Muslim is completely our brother, an exaggeration of our best selves. The difficulty comes in the third part when he deals with the Hindus. Hinduphobia was, of course, a more characteristic response of the British who from the time James Mill published *The History of British India* in 1819 were continually articulating their ambivalence about their Indian connection.

Figure 5. Engraving from S. Augustus Mitchell's *Mitchell's School Geography: A System of Modern Geography* (1867). The illustration ranks societies from "savage" to "civilized and enlightened," placing the United States and Western Europe at the top of a racialized hierarchy.[44]

LESSON XXXVIII.

9. The′o·ry, an explanation.
9. Or′i-gin, source, or cause.
9. Ev′i-dence, proof, testimony.
9. Found′ed, based, established.

20. Va′por, steam, mist, fog.
21. Ef-fect′, the result of a cause
35. Con-clude′, to infer.
45. As-cend′, to go up, to rise.

Articulate properly *rm* and *ng* in *warm′ing* ; *sts* in *mists* ; *nd* in *ground, as-cend′,* *kind* ; *ld* in *told, cold* ; *gr* in *grows, ground,* &c.

THE THEORY OF RAIN. — *A Dialogue.*

[This dialogue between Dr. Duff, a missionary to India, and a Hindoo youth, shows, in a striking manner, how the principles of science are made the means of convincing the heathen of the falsity of their religious systems, and the truth of Christianity.]

1. *Dr. Duff.* What is rain ?
2. *Hindoo.* Water from the sky.

Figure 6. Teacher lesson plan from S. Town and N. M. Holbrook's *The Progressive Third Reader* (1857).[45]

If you know children (or people), you'll know that storytelling is one of the most powerful ways to reach them. Elementary school teachers have long known and used stories as a way of imparting information to their young students. The Theory of Rain was one such story, where Dr. Alexander Duff, a missionary to India, helps a Hindoo child realize that his community's worship of their false god defies his own observations about rain. In this manner, Duff successfully convinces the Hindoo child that his religion is false, and that Christianity is the true religion.

A few foundational assumptions were inscribed within representations of Hindus and Hinduism (and how it paled in comparison to Protestantism) in American education at time. We can think of this as the Master Narrative about Hinduism.

These were taught both implicitly and explicitly through geography textbooks, readers, and through storytelling.

Hinduism Master Narrative

Hinduism was defined by caste oppression, oppression of women, superstitious, backward and often violent rituals, and the need for a Western hand to save it.

There were no alternate representations to illustrate the diversity of perspectives and paths within Hinduism and the Hindu community.

The Protestant religion is compatible with science because of the Enlightenment; Hinduism, on the other hand, isn't compatible with a scientific mindset.

Hinduism is an important example of Heathenism and is far removed from the ideals of American democracy and society as anything else on earth. If the principles of American citizenship are morality, reason, and civic participation, (representations of) Hinduism are to be as far removed from those principles as possible.

But there was hope for the lost Hindoo child. According to Mitchell:

> The great efforts which are now making by various missionary societies for introducing Christianity into India, have in many instances obtained a rich

reward. Hundreds of Hindoos have renounced their gods, the Ganges, and their priests, and have shaken from their limbs the iron chain of caste. A large number of converted natives have in some sense become missionaries, and have been the instruments of turning many to a purer and more enlightened faith. All the societies engaged in the work of missions, have far more calls for labourers than they have instruments at their disposal. Twenty times the number of missionaries, catechists, and schoolmasters, are wanting, and there is abundant evidence that, through the exertions now in progress, the fabric of Hindoo superstition is beginning to totter.[46]

To save the Hindoos from their heathen proclivities, they had to be converted and molded into the American Protestant image. This was an exact replica of the concept behind the Native American boarding schools. The only difference was that—at least at the time—it remained the work of American missionaries, as Hindus hadn't yet landed in the United States.

(Actually, there was one prominent Hindu who did visit the United States from India at the end of the 19th century. But we'll get to that in Chapter Seven!)

When Hindu children *did* begin arriving in American schools in the middle of the 20th century, the Master Narrative had long been embedded in the American psyche and in American textbooks. Representations of Hinduism were reductive and narrow and seemingly at odds with American democracy. As we'll see in chapters and vignettes throughout this book, this hidden curriculum of killing the Hindu to save the American is a thread that continues to the present day.

The framing of Hinduism as antithetical to reason and scientific temperament has deep roots in American education, reaching back to its earliest textbooks. Such narratives ignore centuries of inquiry, debate, and philosophical exploration at the heart of the tradition. The next story brings us into the home of a Hindu American father and son whose lives and minds naturally integrate spiritual and scientific curiosity, analysis, and wonder as natural companions.

Keshav and Arjun: Inquiry and Dharma

Arjun, a college senior, grew up surrounded by that expectation of inquiry. In ninth-grade world-history class, Hinduism appeared only in a single sidebar about caste. At lunch, he realized that for some of his classmates, this brief mention had become the entire lens through which they viewed his tradition. "I don't think being a Hindu was even an identity in our school. It was just not known," Arjun said. The omission bothered him, not so much for what it said, but for what it left out—centuries of philosophical debate, skepticism, and intellectual play.

He began seeking his own sources and found a powerful corrective in ancient Hindu texts known as the Mahāvākyas of the Upaniṣads. Four short sentences sent him "into the rabbit hole." "Because I was interested in science and the nature in consciousness … when I found that they provided a description and that these descriptions agreed with a lot of what modern science was saying, that really fascinated me," he said.

For Arjun, the idea that spiritual texts could converse with physics did not feel exotic. It felt familiar. Small household rituals—never touching a book with one's feet, pausing before Sarasvatī[47]—had always signaled that knowledge itself was sacred. "It really took my own efforts and questioning, critical questioning, but not with an agenda … It's genuine inquiry. And that's been the foundation of Hinduism for its entire existence, which is a beautiful thing."

By contrast, Keshav, Arjun's father, came to value genuine inquiry in a different way through the stories he heard as a child in Karnataka, his graduate studies in semiconductor research, and his move to the U.S. in 1998. His favorite example of how wonder travels is a memory from a corporate Christmas party. His wife had worn a peacock-blue sari, and it caught the attention of the entire ballroom. "All the women who were there, they were so excited to see her peacock-colored sari! They were very appreciative and we felt so good about that." For Keshav, the moment underscored two truths: Americans respond warmly to color and confidence, and inquiry often begins with the simplest question: What are you wearing?

"Each soul craves for the truth, the beauty, the goodness," Keshav tells me. "It's continuous cycles and a transmigration of the soul toward the utmost truth or reality or God, or whatever you call it." When I interview Keshav from his East Bay study, his manner was calm, reflective, and quietly passionate, the mind of an engineer turning over questions of metaphysics. I had just finished speaking with his son, Arjun, and the connection between them—generational, intellectual, and spiritual—was clear.

In their home, father and son often circled the same questions from opposite ends of the dinner table. Where does consciousness start? How far can empirical science reach? Is doubt an act of devotion? Keshav framed these conversations in the language of Dharma—not as rigid obligation, but as situational integrity, the right action for the moment at hand. Arjun preferred the vocabulary of hypotheses and data. Yet both agreed that a mind unwilling to question is a mind unprepared to see.

These habits of thought eventually reached beyond the family dining room and into public life. When California's draft social-science framework once again reduced Hinduism to caste, both Keshav and Arjun felt the tug of responsibility. Arjun testified before the state board, not to preach theology but to call for intellectual accuracy. Said Arjun: "I realized I kind of reflected on my responsibilities as a citizen and my civic duties … Hinduism was the only one that was targeted."

Keshav, who had never been drawn to public speaking, recognized that silence would accomplish nothing. He began coaching other parents on how to distill complex ideas into two-minute statements. "Being an immigrant, you are usually more concerned … anywhere with civic participation, you can't bring change, and you can't beat the hundredth shot of a hammer by skipping the first 99 shots."

The hearings were important, but neither man saw them as the endpoint. Asked later what it means to live as a Hindu American, Arjun spoke in terms of synthesis: "To be proud of where you come from … integrating all the positive things that America has given to us with also the cultural ideas and traditions … and not feeling inferior."

Keshav placed the struggle on a longer arc of history. "I feel the California textbook hearings are going to have a magnitude of impact, a domino effect … In that sense, it is a part of the history of the diaspora." His sense of connection between present action and long-term consequence echoed the same worldview he had described in his study—the soul's continuous journey toward truth.

The throughline for both is not a tally of victories or defeats in policy battles, but the open-ended discipline that led them to speak out in the first place. Inquiry, rooted in both Sanskrit verse and laboratory habit, links a grandmother's *shlokas* (sacred verses), graduate seminars, Bay-Area biotech labs, and a teenager's deep dive into consciousness studies. Any curriculum that treats Hinduism as static misses that kinetic core. Any democracy that celebrates free thought should recognize it.

Hours pass easily in their home. The air is full of thoughtful exchange, generous listening, and an easy hospitality that makes time feel both full and unhurried. There is no performance here—just sincerity, reflection, and an openness to ideas. It is a space where family warmth and intellectual curiosity are not competing values but the same impulse, expressed in different registers.

Keshav's closing words, as I prepare to leave, stay with me long after I get into my car: "Hindu Americans have a historical contribution to make for the betterment of America."

They are words that resist being flattened into slogans or sound bites. They come from a family where questions are as valued as answers, where identity is lived in the interplay between science and scripture, where being Hindu and being American are not separate paths but one road with many points of entry. It is this quality—the quiet, unshakable conviction that truth seeking is a civic as well as a spiritual act—that makes their home feel like part of the same moral landscape described in the previous chapter: a democracy strengthened by those who ask, and keep asking, "What does it mean to be?"

CHAPTER THREE

Immigration and American Public Education

Immigration, Religion, Assimilation, and Education, 1800–1965

Immigrants arrived on the shores of the new United States from around the world, bringing an incredible range of religious practices: Indigenous (or primary), Jewish, Christian, and Muslim (sometimes because of histories of colonization), and sometimes syncretic, or a melding of religious traditions.[48] In fact, the religious diversity in the first centuries of the United States is far beyond the scope of how most of us imagine it to have been. This isn't to suggest that all of these traditions were uniformly respected by the communities of the religious majority—but they were here!

Mexico had been colonized by the Spanish since the 1500s. This meant that the overwhelming majority of Mexican immigrants to the United States from the 1800s were Roman Catholic with generations-long traditions of festivals, saints, and family life that was centered around church and faith.

Because Catholicism in many rural parts of Mexico had blended over centuries with local Indigenous customs, immigrants from those areas often practiced a form of Catholicism that included indigenous rituals, symbols, and communal traditions.[49] U.S. Census data and immigration records estimate that approximately 100,000 Mexican immigrants entered the U.S. between 1900 and 1920. Many settled in the American Southwest and worked in railroads and agriculture.

For similar reasons, the vast majority (roughly 90 percent) of immigrants from other parts of Latin America were also Roman Catholic, including those from Cuba, Puerto Rico, and Haiti. At the same time, syncretic faiths, like Santeria practiced by Afro-Cuban Cuba, blended Indigenous practices with Catholicism. Similarly, while nearly all Haitians identified as Catholic, Voodoo was widely practiced in rural and Afro-Haitian communities. Jamaica was the outlier in the Caribbean when it came to faith. Due to British colonial influence, the majority (approximately 94 percent) of Jamaican immigrants practiced some form of Protestantism. In total, U.S. Census Bureau records indicate that anywhere between 250,000 and 500,000 people immigrated from Latin America and the Caribbean to the U.S. between 1850 and 1920.

Immigrants from Canada reflected an interesting mix. English-speaking immigrants were mainly Protestant, while the French-speaking were mostly Roman Catholic. According to the U.S. Census Bureau, about 750,000 Canadians entered the U.S. between 1900 and 1920.

Immigrants from the Ottoman Empire were predominantly (90–95 percent) Maronite Catholic, Eastern Orthodox, and Melkite Greek Catholic; the remainder were Muslim or

Druze—an offshoot of Ismaili Islam that originated in the 11th century in what is now Lebanon, Syria, and Northern Israel, which eventually took on a distinct philosophy and culture. Approximately 110,000 immigrants arrived from the region from 1870 to the early 1920s. Voluntary migration from Sub-Saharan Africa was very small—less than 1,000 immigrants between 1800 and 1920.[50] Their religious affiliation was mixed—some were Muslim, others Christian, and others practiced traditional African religions.[51]

Immigration from Asia

Chinese immigrants had largely met the labor demand from the California Gold Rush and the Transcontinental Railroad construction during the mid-19th century; Chinese immigrants were also taking up roles in agriculture, mining, and domestic and laundry services. Nearly all Chinese immigrants to the United States in the 19th century came from rural counties of Guangdong Province,[52] and most were working-class men speaking Cantonese or Taishanese (a Chinese language variety). Religious life among these communities was often syncretic, blending Confucian, Taoist, and folk religious practices.[53] Some Chinese immigrants, under pressure or from mission schools, converted to Christianity, but many retained their traditional beliefs. The Chinese Exclusion Act of 1882 was the first major federal immigration policy restricting immigration on the basis of nationality; it also denied U.S. Citizenship to Chinese immigrants already living in the United States.

Due to political upheaval in Japan (i.e., the Meiji Restoration), Japanese immigration to the U.S. rose in the late 19th and early 20th centuries, largely to Hawaiian sugar plantations and later to farms on the West Coast of the continental U.S., particularly in California. These migrants primarily practiced Buddhism or Shintoism; some had converted to Protestantism before immigration due to American missionary work in Japan, but this was a small minority. In fact, Japanese Buddhist temples became central community institutions in Hawaii[54] and California.[55] The Buddhist Churches of America was formed in the 1890s to serve Japanese immigrants. However, an informal agreement with the Japanese government in 1907 meant they would no longer grant passports to U.S-bound laborers. And the California Alien Lands Laws (in 1913 and 1920) prevented Japanese immigrants from owning land.

Koreans began migrating to the U.S. in small waves in 1903, following the Japanese occupation of Korea. Some were seeking to advance Korean independence from abroad. Most Korean immigrants practiced a mix of Buddhism, Confucianism, and Korean shamanic traditions (Musok).[56] Christian Korean immigrants, who had been converted by American missionaries, were afraid of being targeted by the Korean monarchy and then by the Japanese colonial authorities. Korean Christians, already connected with the American missionary network, were amongst the earliest Korean immigrants to the United States.

After the U.S. colonization of the Philippines in 1898, Filipinos were considered American nationals (not citizens), making immigration relatively easy. After 300 years of Spanish colonization, the majority of Filipinos were Roman Catholic, although some, in more rural areas of the Philippines, retained their Indigenous beliefs. That is, until the Tydings-McDuffie Act of 1934, which reclassified Filipinos as aliens, creating an annual immigration quota of 50.

Sikh men from Punjab, arriving between 1900 and 1917, made up 90 percent[57] of the earliest Indian immigrants to the U.S.[58] They worked mostly as agricultural laborers or in the lumber and rail industries. Most Sikhs settled in the California region, although a small number settled in New York City, including Harlem.[59] Most maintained their traditional faith, although a small number had been converted by American Presbyterian missionaries. The remaining immigrants were mostly Muslim, with a small number of Hindus. However, all of this came to a halt with the Immigration Acts of 1917 and 1924, which created an Asiatic Barred Zone.

Country/ Region	Est. Immigrants (1882–1917)	Foreign Born in U.S. by 1910	Notes
China	Minimal (decline after 1882)	~94,000	The Chinese Exclusion Act (1882) drastically reduced immigration.
Japan	~150,000–200,000	~170,000	Immigration surged until the 1907 Gentlemen's Agreement.
Korea	~7,000–10,000	Included in "Other"	Migration began in 1903, mostly to Hawaii plantations.
Philippines	~1,000–5,000	~5,600 (by 1920)	Filipinos were U.S. nationals; a small but growing presence.
India	~4,000–6,000	2,545	Mostly Punjabi Sikhs; immigration ended with the 1917 Barred Zone.

Figure 7. Asian Immigration According to the U.S. Census between 1882 and 1917

Immigration from Europe

The largest flows of immigration to the United States during the 19th and early 20th centuries originated in Europe. Between 1880 and 1914, more than 20 million Europeans arrived in what would later be described as the "Great Wave." The largest single religious group was Roman Catholic, with immigrants arriving from Italy, Ireland, and Poland. Jews, who were escaping

Russian pogroms, formed the largest group of non-Christian immigrants; more than 2 million Jews arrived in the U.S. during this period. While the vast majority of European immigrants prior to 1880 were Protestant, they now constituted less than 40 percent of Europeans arriving in the United States. Catholic and Eastern Orthodox Christian immigrants, despite being Christian, were often depicted as outsiders who threatened the Protestant values of American democracy.

By 1910 nearly 15 percent of the U.S. population—more than 13 million people—was foreign-born. This was worrisome to pockets of Americans, whose concerns about job security and the health of American society were exacerbated by the aftereffects of World War I —which were exacerbated further a decade later with the arrival of The Great Depression. Immigration restriction laws in 1921 and 1924 set large-scale immigration limits for the first time in the nation's history. These policies severely restricted immigration from Eastern and Southern Europe (1921). The Asian Exclusion provision in the Johnson-Reed Act of 1924 effectively banned immigration from Asia.[60]

But the folks who immigrated before those policies took hold were already here!

By 1911, more than half (57.5 percent) of the children in the public schools of 37 of the largest American cities were of foreign-born parentage; in the parochial schools of 24 of these 37 cities, the children of foreign-born parents constituted 63.5 percent of the total registration.[61] And by 1911 almost 50 percent of the students in secondary schools were of foreign-born parentage.[62]

These large demographic shifts presented urban public school teachers with a new challenge: educating immigrant children.

This included the important task of assimilating the students into American society, even (and sometimes, especially) if that meant distancing children from their families' culture, language, customs, and habits. Immigrant families often lived in diaspora enclaves within these cities where they collectively migrated the customs of the home country, creating a continuity of home culture and social organization. School was the portal into "American life," and school was entrusted with ensuring these children would become valuable, productive members of society.

> Our task is to break—their groups and
> settlements, to assimilate or amalgamate
> these people as a part of the American race,
> and to implant in their children, so far as
> can be done, the Anglo-Saxon conception
> of rightiousness [righteousness-sic] law,
> order, and popular government, and to
> awaken in them reverance for our democratic
> institutions and for those things which we as
> people hold to be of abiding worth.
>
> – Ellwood P. Cubberley, *Changing
> Conceptions of Education,* 1909

This was not without its obstacles.

First, cities often had insufficient seats to meet the needs of the mandatory schooling policy. Once these were created, they discovered that many of the children were overaged for their grades, as they had missed years of schooling. This meant that a classroom might have students from across a broad age range; a one-size-fits-all approach to curriculum would be ineffective.

Then there was the issue of language. While the classes were all taught in English, there were an enormous number of children who spoke another language, all in the same classroom.

Even so, immigration was seen as a "one-generation problem." The hypothesis was that if the children were successfully assimilated into society through the schools—if schools did their job well—there would be an upstream effect on parents, thereby solving another social challenge—creating a unified populace that shared American values and habits. Schools were designed to do very little to support immigrant parents, relying instead on this kind of magical thinking.

> The concept of Americanization was based upon the assumption that foreigners and foreign ideas and ways were a threat to American political, economic, social stability, and security. The infiltration of foreign culture, it was feared, would eventually bring about a deterioration of the American "way of life." Programs were designed, therefore, to suppress or eliminate all that was conceived of as "foreign" and to impose upon the immigrant a cultural uniformity with an American pattern."[63]

Scholars note that hygiene education was a focus in school, particularly for immigrant children. There was a particular concept that immigrants were inherently dirty and disease-ridden, not just as a result of their circumstances. We see strains of this viral mentality today.

My children both attended a highly respected, progressive public elementary school in Brooklyn, New York. It was late in the winter of 2017, and my 5th grader and his class did a study of New York immigration, centered largely around Ellis Island and the early part of the 20th century. In late March, they were to put on an immigration musical. Having witnessed this same play the year before (because my other son is a year older), I began to have an uneasy feeling that some of the feedback I had shared had gone unheard.

Then we received an email from his teachers, with a note from the dance teacher who was coordinating the costumes for the play, which included the following:

> Go into a closet or a drawer and find something old and make it look older—soak in tea or coffee, or take out to the park and dirty it up, or beat it up in some way.
>
> POVERTY-WEAR!!!!
>
> Use wine corks (if you indulge in such things) and burn the ends of them and bring on show day to smudge up their faces and arms etc. ... dark eye makeup will work for this as well.

I was taken aback by this. Surely, we were not directing students to associate dirtiness with immigrant identity! This spiraled into a series of email exchanges, which I hesitatingly initiated, among the class teachers and parents. (As a doctoral student in education at the time, I intentionally gave my kids' teachers extra space, as I knew I was prone to over analysis!) Some parents agreed with me, others found my "woke agenda" noxious and ahistorical. One white, Dutch father then took it upon himself to privately send this email to me and another father who had also disagreed with the teachers suggested costume attire.

> Dear A and Indu,
>
> You seem to suggest the drama teachers act as racists. Since you have sent since your mails to a large group of parents it has now become a humiliating public trial of the teachers.
>
> Your effort to rewrite American history out of political correctness would be funny if it was not so insulting to my kids and me. Tomorrow they will perform an innocent 5th grade play, and yes, in dirty clothes. Not because we are racists, the paradigm you are now trying to create toward the poor 5th graders, their parent and their drama teachers, but in all innocence as they are fully aware the dirt was caused by the conditions on the immigrant ships.
>
> Personally, I would have compassion with people that got dirty from long travels and the implicit suggestion that dirty people could not have dignity is awkward to me.
>
> I am not happy with your efforts to bring political activism in the classroom of our kids.
>
> Kind regards,
>
> JP (father of J and recent immigrant)

This parent was a C-suite hire working for a multinational bank. He seemed to miss the point about messaging versus historical accuracy. In the end, nothing changed about the play. I responded to the group with the following email:

> It seems to be a particularly significant moment in America, from our family's perspective, to reframe notions of immigration, and to consider and critique the ways in which we imagine and represent immigrants, symbolically and narratively. The issue with stereotypes is not that they are always false; it's that they are a sliver of the truth presented as a much larger portion of reality, often obscuring the other really significant facts and experiences of an individual or a group of people. The human mind experiences role-play differently than it does a discussion or a reading. These experiences leave lasting impressions in the formative years of young minds. So, our family has decided to represent an immigrant with great consideration of his dignity and wealth of spirit. A will come dressed in some approximation of early 20th-century clothing that is washed and neatly pressed, and his face will be clean.

This is not to suggest that all educators were solely concerned with assimilation when it came to educating immigrant children. From 1903 until her death in 1912, Julia Richman, district superintendent in New York City School Districts 2 and 3 experimented with **differentiation**, an individualized approach to teaching and promoting students. Between 1908 and 1922, she wrote about her increased awareness of the importance of community connection and support.[64] Other NYC district superintendents in Division I (south of 14th

Street, the neighborhoods of many diaspora communities in Manhattan), experimented with teaching English as a second language, with some incorporating classes specifically for immigrant children to learn English and bring them to grade level. "The most ambitious of the constructs devised was the large-scale introduction of special classes by Julia Richman throughout the school districts under her governance. These efforts by Julia Richman are worthy of special note."[65]

Richman's efforts reflected a broader movement among progressive educators of the time. William Maxwell, superintendent of New York City schools from 1898 to 1917, likewise championed reforms that addressed the practical needs of immigrant and poor children—introducing school lunches, student baths, and vacation schools that provided nourishment, hygiene, and enrichment beyond the regular school year:

> Superintendent William Maxwell felt deeply about the suffering of the poor. He knew that thousands of children came hungry to school each day and that stomach pains gnawed at them as they tried to study; he thought providing cheap lunches in schools the "most pressing of all school reforms." He proudly told of a principal on the lower east side who was so loved and respected that as she picked her way through the crowds and the pushcarts on the street, children smiled at her, older boys tipped their caps, and bearded men greeted her. He helped to install baths in schools so that children who had no water in their flats could get clean. He marveled at the ability of teachers who instructed pupils who could speak no English; in one school alone there

were twenty-nine different languages or dialects. He stayed in the city during the steaming summer months partly to encourage those teaching in the vacation schools, where hundreds of thousands of children went voluntarily to learn crafts and nature study. Maxwell told with delight about a little girl, Leah, who invited her teacher home to eat at a table set just like the one in the picture in a magazine her teacher had lent to her.[66]

It's important to note in this discussion that while mandatory education had been codified into law for decades, this did not mean that all children had access to the same—or even similar—education in terms of content, approaches to teaching and learning, and material resources. State-sponsored schools remained segregated by race, especially in the South, but also through de facto segregation in the North, shaped by housing discrimination, redlining (discriminatory race-based housing practices), and school district zoning. School curricula continued to center white, Protestant, Anglo-American identity as the standard, continuing to teach the hierarchy of cultures from the previous centuries, even if implicitly so.

Textbooks and classrooms reinforced a nationalism that papered over the complexity of immigrant experiences, the violence of slavery and colonization, or the contributions of non-European peoples. Meanwhile, school facilities for Black, Indigenous, immigrant, and poor children were often overcrowded, underfunded, understaffed, and under-resourced.

Schools, it turns out, were not the great equalizer of American society. Instead, they were kind of like the plaque disclosing tablets they distributed in public schools during dental hygiene presentations when I was a kid. As you chewed on the little pink squares, the parts of your teeth with plaque would turn pink, while the parts that were plaque-free would not. Schools revealed the progress *and* the remaining challenges in American society—our social health—beneath the intention and rhetoric of universal schooling and civic education.

As we'll explore in the next chapter, the American Civil Rights movement would play a huge role in shifting the paradigm of public education.

We were continuing to strive for a more perfect union.

Holy Cow

The phrase "Holy cow," a common American exclamation of surprise, may actually have roots in Hinduism. Some linguists and cultural historians argue that the expression entered American English in the late 19th and early 20th centuries as a playful nod to the sacred status of cows in Hindu tradition. With increased immigration from South Asia and growing awareness of India through British colonial literature and global travel, Hindu ideas (however misunderstood or exoticized) entered popular discourse. The phrase likely became popularized through American comic books and baseball slang, but its deeper origins may lie in the American encounter with Hindu beliefs—suggesting that Hinduism has long existed in American culture in subtle, surprising ways.

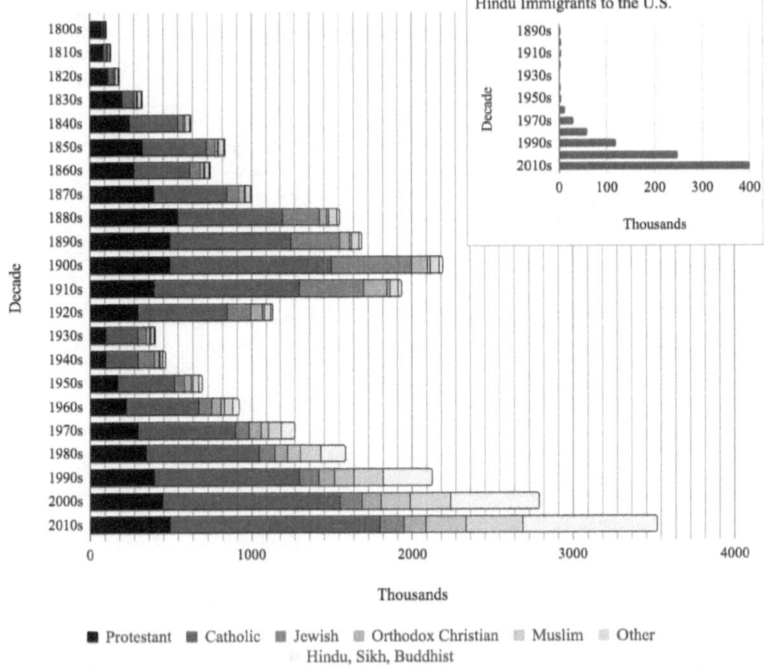

Figure 8. Immigration to the United States by Religious Group between 1800 and 2010.[67]

*Because religious affiliation wasn't systematically recorded in immigration records during this period, the numbers are inferred based on country of origin, historical religious demographics, and known migration patterns. This chart should be read as interpretive rather than definitive, especially for the smaller or marginalized religious traditions. (Sources that helped determine these estimates can be found in the Endnotes.)

You'll notice a category entitled "Other" in the graph above. Other is, as always, a vast and very interesting group. Here is what happens when we unzip that category by dominant years of immigration flow. As you can see in the table below, there was an incredibly rich diversity of religions in the United States.

Years	
1800s-1840s[68]	Native American spiritual traditions; African traditional religions (via Caribbean); Mennonites, Hutterites, Shakers; Freemasons (moral/spiritual philosophy); Spiritualists (seances, mediums); Unitarians and Universalists
1850s–1870s[69]	Santería (Afro-Cuban syncretism); Voodoo (Haitian syncretism); Espiritismo (Puerto Rican/Cuban spiritualism); Christian Science (Mary Baker Eddy); Swedenborgians; Theosophists (esoteric spiritualism)
1880s–1910s[70]	Obeah and Myalism (Afro-Jamaican); Jehovah's Witnesses; Seventh-day Adventists; Agnostics, Freethinkers; Rosicrucians
1920s–1950s[71]	Bahá'ís (from Iran, very rare); Secular Jews and Christians; Jain immigrants (if present, likely miscategorized); Humanists; Small numbers of Parsis (Zoroastrians)
1960s-2010s[71]	Traditional African religions; Caribbean syncretic faiths; Jains; Zoroastrians; Bahá'ís; unaffiliated/secular; Chinese folk religions; Yazidis; Druze; various syncretic movements; Indigenous spiritualities from outside the U.S.

Figure 9. U.S. Immigration of Other Religious Groups by Year

Religion and Assimilation into American Society

When it comes to faith, religion is not always evenly respected and appreciated and understood in the same way by all people. If you are an immigrant or an Indigenous person or a descendant of formerly enslaved people but you have faith in common with the majority of Americans, that is a pretty powerful mechanism for social acceptance. So, while an Indian Christian might be a religious minority in their home country, once they arrive here, they are a part of the majority religious group (especially if they are connected to an American missionary network), and there isn't an inherent suspicion of their morality and belonging because of their *faith*.

Prominent American sociologists Nancy Foner and Richard Alba note that there is sparse academic analysis of immigration and religion in the U.S. This is, in part, because scholars rely on data collected by government agencies, which are not permitted to collect information about religion. But they also argue that religion is not perceived as a barrier to acculturation in the U.S. (in contrast with Europe). They note a "positive gloss on religion's role among today's newcomers," pointing to research which finds that Americans have a particularly high level of belief and religiosity as compared to other economically prosperous societies. They also point to the *functionality* of religion in meeting the social needs of immigrants—refuge, respectability, and resources.

In their book *Immigrant Religion in the U.S. and Western Europe: Bridge or Barrier to Inclusion?* Foner and Alba state, "To be sure, one way this Americanization happens is by conversion to Christianity because of its charter status in American society. For instance, the proportion of Christians among Asian immigrants to the United States is generally much higher than is the case in their countries of origin. To some extent, this may be the result of selective immigration by those who were already Christian in the homeland. But there can be little doubt that, for other immigrants, the move to America involves conversion to Christianity."[72]

The other day, I was having dinner with a Chinese American friend. Her great-great-grandfather had immigrated from China to San Francisco in the middle of the 19th century. I shared that I was writing about immigration flows from across Asian countries from the perspective of nationality and religion. I asked her if she knew what religion her grandfather had practiced. She shared that, as far as she had been told by her father and uncles, her grandfather wasn't particularly religious. But he owned a Bible and belonged to a church community because he was a "practical man" and being part of a church in America was a "means to an end." It meant learning English and having a social connection to being American. "The Bible and Sunday School meant Christian, but funerals and weddings in our family did not accord with Christian practices," she said. A few days later she confirmed that they followed Buddhist practices.

Seventy-five percent of U.S. immigrants are Christian or convert to Christianity. This eases acculturation and acceptance and can nurture an intragroup empathy that cuts through racial tension. I encourage you to pay attention to news stories and social media posts where a person of color is telling a story about racial discrimination but references their Christian faith to establish their relatability and morality and signal that they deserve empathy. This is not a critique of those people. It makes sense for someone who comes from a racial or ethnic minority to make a personal connection with the ethnic majority. It is good storytelling! And, of course, practicing Christians do deserve empathy!

But doesn't everyone?

As we discussed in previous chapters, there is a lot more complexity to the story of U.S. religion than Protestant or Christian dominance. Remember the hierarchy of religions in the earlier days of public education? Well, it seems to offer some transcendence over race, ethnicity, or nationality. The degree to which it helps varies over time and is vulnerable to geopolitical context, but it does make a difference.

I want to make a quick pitstop before we move on to contemporary (1965 onward) representations of Hinduism in American public school.

Let's talk about language.

The Rain in Spain

Remember the focus educators put on English language acquisition in the early 20th century during the "Great Wave." In fact, English language acquisition continues to be a primary focus when it comes to teaching immigrant children. When I was doing my literature review for my doctoral dissertation, the majority of research on teaching immigrant children was about teaching them English. The majority of research on U.S. immigrant teachers was about their English language fluency. There was very little (shockingly little) research about the capacities and knowledges of immigrant children and teachers and what they might add to—and not just need from—classrooms. Now, of course, this is a very important capacity to develop in students (and immigrant teachers). We are an English-speaking nation, and even in schools that encourage and support bilingualism, English is necessary. We would be doing the vast majority of K-12 immigrant students a disservice if we did not teach them to be confident English speakers.

Most Hindu immigrants come to the U.S. from India. The majority of those immigrants arrive already fluent in English, thanks to the former British colonization and the education system they left behind in 1947. (If you're not familiar with Macaulay's *Minute on Indian Education*, I recommend looking it up!). They can speak, read, and write in English.

However …

An established and growing body of research shows that *accent* plays a large role in social acceptance in the U.S. People tend to favor speakers who share their accent.[73] Non-standard (i.e., American) accents are linked to perceptions of incompetence or inauthenticity.[74] An accent can lead to worse hiring outcomes, even if the applicant is fluent in English.[75] Accents can create a cognitive processing delay or difference—in other words, the listener takes longer to respond or responds differently to accented speech than speech in standard English, even if the speaker is clear.[76] The "right" (i.e., Standard American) accent acts as a trust marker for social grouping.[77] A non-American accent while speaking even fluent English is seen as a permissible basis for social exclusion compared to race and religion.[78]

Accent is more than a communication barrier or something that is made fun of on *The Simpsons*. It shapes perceptions of credibility, belonging, and identity perception.[79] This is why people learn to code switch or change their accent or style of speaking or mannerisms to match that of the group they are in to be accepted and seen as trustworthy. They don't even need to have read the research. If you have strong social awareness and read social cues, it can be fairly obvious. It's important to remember that code switching is not about being inauthentic so much as it is about intuiting what is the most effective way to be successful in social interactions.

It's important for all of us—families, educators, community members, and leaders—to pause and think about both accents and code switching when we make assumptions about how we perceive and are being perceived. This is not about being apologetic or offended, but about simply having greater awareness so we can continue to co-construct rich, warm, welcoming, and inclusive communities and schools. This is especially pertinent to parent advocacy regarding curriculum, as the majority of Hindu American parents are immigrants and speak fluent, but often accented, English when they raise concerns about *what* is being taught about Hinduism in their children' s schools.

In the U.S., many immigrant communities live their faith openly, carrying religious identity with ease. Religious communities can, in fact, ease acculturation. In the next story, we meet Vaijayanthi and her father, Akshay, who notice something different for Hindu Americans. While they themselves are comfortable expressing their Hinduness, they see many other Hindus choosing silence, even when peers from other faiths speak about their religiosity with pride. In their view, some Hindu Americans feel a particular pressure to recede, a pressure that often comes not from outsiders, but from within the community itself.

Vaijayanthi and Akshay: Hinduism in the Open

When I stayed in the Bay Area for interviews, the second half of my trip was spent under Akshay's roof. The house was always full—full of voices, food, and people coming and going. They seemed to feed half the neighborhood without effort. There was prayer every day, a rhythm set not by obligation but by devotion, and laughter was as much a part of the household soundscape as the clink of plates or the hum of conversation.

Akshay's daughter Vaijayanthi shared with me about her transition to middle school. "When they were having … this thing in the quad where different clubs would try to bring in new members, I heard this group of Indian girls walking by and they were like, 'Oh my God, that's so embarrassing,'" Vaijayanthi said. "I would never join. And that's where it kind of hit me like, oh, this is not the same as middle school. This is really different."

Vaijayanthi's voice holds both surprise and disappointment as she recounts the moment. She is in high school now, best friends with Yagnee—who appeared earlier in this book—their families bound by years of closeness. Her father, Akshay, was best friends with Yagnee's father. The bond between the two families is not simply friendly; it is woven into their daily lives. Vaijayanthi is pensive as she talks about her school. "I think they want to fit in because at least from my experience, I think more than non-Indian people, Indian people are more against Hinduism and their own culture. I don't know why—it happens a lot."

She tells me how she wears a bindi to school every day. In the first few weeks of school, she would take it off in the bathroom. No one had said anything unkind, but she felt the need to blend in. "I just personally felt like, oh, what if people … not dislike me, but think I'm—I don't know. It just felt … I don't know how to put it into words. But I guess as the year progressed, I realized no one really thinks about it in a bad way, and I just didn't take it off after that. But sometimes I do feel like I stand out."

What she notices most is the contrast between her peers' willingness to share their religious identity. "I feel like all of the other clubs, religious clubs at school, do a lot more. And then I feel like all of the people in our school who are of different religions, they're really proud of their religion. And even though there's a good amount of Indians in our school that are Hindu, they never mention their religion. For Diwali, me and one other girl dressed up—nobody else dressed up. Even my close friends said that they were kind of embarrassed or uncomfortable to do that. So it kind of sometimes feels like, I wish people were more brave."

She thinks of her Muslim friend at another school, where there are few Muslims. "She tells people about her religion. She's very open about it. So, I wish people were more brave to not be embarrassed ... I wish we had more people who were braver about their religion."

When her father, Akshay came to the U.S. as a young man, he arrived first in upstate New York and found it isolating. "In the first two or three months, I would feel like, oh my God, this is such a lonely place. I come from a place—although it's a village—it's like a lot of people around and a social ecosystem," Akshay said. "And this was like, oh my God, where are people? ... I saw super isolation at a grand level, mega level."

The natural beauty struck him—especially in northern New York—but so did the separation he saw in people's lives. "People were already in their own pockets." The experience was not defined by religion but by the awareness of being visibly different.

"I definitely felt as a person of Indian origin ... once in a while you would come across some harsh local people ... particularly white people, and they would look to treat you in a different manner," he said. "At the time, I don't think I was equipped enough to really handle that in an improvised manner. Those days it was more of 'I'm so much an outsider here and everybody else around me is so local, so I need to be mindful of my actions.' So, I was overly aware. That was a heavy burden, which was not necessary."

In time, the questions about his religion began to appear. "There are two types of people I know—people who would be, Hey, why don't you eat cows? And … Have you found Jesus? Those kinds of questions. Definitely two different layers of questions."

Akshay remembers the first time he felt the need to prepare his eldest child for the way Hinduism might be misrepresented in school. "Before she even hit middle school. And to me that was such a burden on her. She doesn't deserve that. I remember my own childhood—I was still playing games and everything." But he knew if he didn't explain, the first lesson she learned about her own tradition might be wrong.

This readiness to teach has extended beyond his own family. When a textbook in his children's school misrepresented Hinduism, he went in to speak to the class. The teacher was open and welcoming, and Akshay was able to share what he knew, offering the students a fuller picture than the book provided.

> Everybody except Hindus are standing
> for their values—and rightfully so, I don't
> have anything against anybody else—but
> then Hindus feel like, oh, they shouldn't be
> getting into this. And to me that is very, very
> disappointing.
>
> – Akshay, talking about
> Hindus in professional spaces

He has seen this contrast with Indian Christians and Indian Muslims, who he says tend to be more forthright about their beliefs. For Akshay, this reticence is tied to a colonial mindset, one that has yet to be shed.

Yet in his own home, the opposite is true. Their daily prayers, their willingness to open their home, their friendships across the community—all of it speaks to a life where identity is not hidden but lived openly. The warmth they met me with every day I stayed with them was not something they turned on for guests; it was simply the way they moved through the world.

Vaijayanthi's observations about her peers, and Akshay's reflections on immigration, faith, and belonging, both circle the same truth: Belonging is not just about who accepts you, but about how willing you are to be known. In a society that celebrates certain kinds of difference and ignores others, the choice to speak, to share, to stand visible in your tradition is not always easy. But in this household, that choice is made daily—not as a statement, but as a way of life.

The Hindu experience of being religious in the U.S. is, in many ways, unlike that of other faith groups. It often means navigating visibility in a culture that knows little about your tradition, balancing the instinct to blend in with the desire to live openly, and finding the courage to be known even when others from your own community choose silence.

CHAPTER FOUR

Contemporary Discourses in American Education

I recently presented a paper on the Vedic (rooted in the Vedas or ancient Hindu scriptures) concept of intuition at the annual meeting of the National Association of Research in Science Teaching. This was my first time attending this event, which meant I was kind of wide-eyed as I wandered the 2,000-person conference, attending a variety of sessions that touched on my emerging research areas and trying to navigate my way around the large convention center near Washington, D.C.

During one session that I attended, one of the professors began her presentation on futures reasoning with the following observations: Every solution we imagine for today's challenges may end up creating a new challenge for tomorrow. When plastics were first introduced, they were seen as an alternative to ivory in everyday products like buttons and piano keys. Plastics became a part of mainstream manufacturing because of ecological concerns. The irony, of course, is that plastics (especially single-use plastics) are a major ecological concern today.

The next morning, I grabbed a coffee in the lobby and started chatting with a bright young woman wearing a whole new color of lanyard. I asked her which conference she was attending. It was the Association of Plastic Recyclers.

Every solution we imagine for today's challenges may end up creating a new challenge for tomorrow.

The U.S. public education system has always been about more than successfully imparting subject information to students. What information should be taught? Who should be taught what? How should they be taught? Why should they be taught? These are not straightforward questions, nor have the answers been clear across American educational history.

The endeavor to harness public education to address broader needs, interests, and aspirations of American society, the American state, and its institutions—for better and for worse—has informed these answers from the early 19th century until today. This inspired Horace Mann and the Common School Era in the mid-1800s. It led to the installation of mandatory, universal education and high school vocational tracks in the second half of the Industrial Revolution. It also led to the development of Native American boarding schools, beginning with the Carlisle School, with devastating consequences.

From the onset of American K-12 public education, the challenge of creating a unified society of upstanding citizens out of a population of unprecedented diversity—across race, ethnicity, religion, class, and origin story—appeared to create a battleground between unity and uniformity, equity and sameness.

There were at least two other significant aspects in the development of American public education that we haven't yet discussed—educational scholarship, including theory *and* empirical research about teaching and learning, and teacher education. It's helpful to pull these threads into our conversation because they help paint a fuller picture of what is going on in schools and classrooms, both behind the scenes and in plain view.

If you grew up outside the U.S. you might not be familiar with this common expression: *Those who can, do. Those who can't, teach.*

The impact of this expression is … well it's rather insulting! But let's move past offense and unpack some of the implicit assumptions:

Teaching is for people who are incapable of doing real work.

Teaching is not an aspirational profession.

Teaching doesn't require any special skill or craft. It is for the skill-less.

As a former classroom teacher, teacher educator, and educational scholar, I have a lot to say about this set of assumptions. It speaks to the history of the teaching profession. It tells us a lot about how people value teachers as a part of society. It can tell us about whether people think schools are successful or not and what role teachers have to play in them. It's no coincidence that, since the Common School Era, most classroom teachers—and even many school principals—have been women. Today, roughly 80 to 90 percent of K–12 teachers are female, while men still hold a disproportionate share of district-level leadership positions such as superintendents, administrators, and deans. In large part, especially with the introduction of textbooks and the standardization of curriculum, teaching has been seen by the public as a technical profession, where the teacher simply delivers the predetermined content, requiring no particular skill or craft.

But teachers are doing so much more than delivering content! And teaching requires so much more than reading out of a textbook or reading off of a PowerPoint.

If you are a fan of the TV show *Schitt's Creek*, you'll remember that hilarious scene where Moira Rose is trying to "teach" her son David how to make enchiladas.

Moira: Yes, so try to keep up. OK, next. Now's the time to sprinkle in the chili pepper flakes.

David: We've already done that.

Moira: What number are we on?

David: Oh my god, is this not your mother's recipe?

Moira: Yes, and now I'm passing it on to you! So, try to keep up. Next step is to fold in the cheese.

David: What does that mean? What does "fold in the cheese" mean?

Moira: You fold it in.

David: I, I understand that, but how, how do you fold it? Do you fold it in half like a piece of paper and drop it in the pot, or what do you do?

Moira: David, I cannot show you everything.

David: OK, well, Moira can you show me one thing?

Moira: You just ... here's what you do. You just fold it in.

David: OK, I don't know how to fold broken cheese like that.

Moira: David, then I don't know how to be any clearer! You take that thing that's in your hand and you ...

David: If you say "fold in" one more time ...

Moira: It says "fold it in"!

David: This is your recipe! You fold in the cheese then!

Moira: Don't you dare!

David: You fold it in!

Moira: David! Oh good, now I see bubbles. David! What does burning smell like?

In other words, teaching, learning, and schools are complex endeavors, far beyond textbooks, and standard, and educational scholarship, and teacher education can help us understand this better.

Educational Scholarship

At the same time that the broad campaigns of public education we have discussed were taking place, there was a thoughtful community of American scholar-practioners of education. Some of the more prolific names from the late 19th and early 20th centuries included John Dewey, William James, Jane Addams, and W. E. B. Du Bois. Educational research was concerned with the theory practice gap; this meant that educational theories were put to the test in classrooms, sometimes even lab classrooms, pioneered by John Dewey. The practical implications of pedagogies were studied as were critical examinations of different teaching policy agendas on students. In 1916, the American Educational Research Association (AERA) was founded. Its mission was: Concerned with improving educational process by encouraging scholarly inquiry related to education and evaluation and by promoting the dissemination and practical application of research results.[80]

According to AERA's website, the association now has approximately 25,000 members of which two-thirds are women, up from 30 percent in 1975–76. About 65 percent of AERA members have PhDs or EdDs; 14 percent of its members reside outside the U.S., representing more than 96 countries. Its annual meeting has an average attendance of more than 13,000 people, making it one of the largest academic conferences in the world, coming just after the American Heart Association. AERA is composed of 12 divisions[81] and 150 Special Interest Groups (SIGs).

Apart from AERA, there are a few other general professional organizations of education research, including the National Center for Education Research (NCER), the American Institute for Research (AIR), and the National Education Association (NEA). In addition to these, several other research groups focus on specializations within the field, including special education, English, mathematics, art, science, and social studies. Some organizations have regional divisions. Most of them not only hold regular meetings but also nurture emergent scholars through professional—and sometimes fiscal—support, and they interact with schools, educators, districts, and educational policymakers.

Which is to say ... education research, which is largely oriented toward applied questions of pedagogy, practice, and policy, is among the largest field of social science scholarship globally. While education research is well-distributed across the world, the U.S. remains one of its most influential centers. As with many domains of American life, what happens in U.S. education has a ripple effect around the world.

Remember that delightful adage from earlier in this chapter, the one about how teaching doesn't really require any skills? Well, one of the more significant findings of education research is that content knowledge does not guarantee or imply **pedagogical content knowledge**. In other words, being an expert in a subject does not mean you automatically know how to *teach* other people about that subject. For educators, teaching is not the same as content delivery. Teaching is a craft. (Although in Moira Rose's case, she neither knew how to make enchiladas nor how to teach David how to make them!)

Teacher Education

Along with the development of a state-sponsored system of education and the establishment of the academic discipline of education, came formalized education for teachers. While in the past teachers were typically volunteers from within the communities[82] who, perhaps, exemplified teacherly dispositions[83] such as patience or "having a way with children" or simply that they showed up!—the professionalization of the teaching profession required something else.

For Common School teachers, this meant normal schools[84] (borrowed from the French *école normale*)—a new project of teacher training institutions. Championed by Horace Mann, the first normal school was established in Massachusetts in 1839, providing lab-based education for teaching candidates who learned about pedagogy in practice from model teachers in model classrooms. It was no longer sufficient for teachers to know the subject matter they were teaching; they were to learn *how* to teach it. Normal schools continued on into the early 20th century where they evolved into four-year teachers' colleges. Starting in the 1910s and 1920s, some institutions began granting bachelor's degrees in education. By the middle of the 20th century, most of these teachers' colleges had become full schools or colleges within mainstream universities. It followed suit that these colleges began offering graduate degrees in education, including master's degrees and doctoral degrees.[85]

The Teaching Profession

Now that teaching had become professionalized, and teacher education had been established as a necessary step in that professionalization, job contracts began to reflect the professional expectations of teachers. (It is very informative, and sometimes entertaining, to look at teacher contracts from the past three centuries.) For the purpose of our conversation, let's take a quick look at one in particular. Since the American education project was concerned with the moral development of the youngest Americans, its schools were focused on the morality of the (mostly female) teaching force. The image below is a teacher's contract from 1923.

TEACHERS CONTRACT 1923

This is an agreement between Miss_______________ teacher, and the Board of Education of the ____________ School, whereby Miss ____________ agrees to reach for a period of eight months, beginning Sept. 1, 1923. The Board of Education agrees to pay Miss ____________ the sum of ($75) per month.

Miss ____________ agrees:

1. Not to get married. This contract becomes null and void immediately if the teacher marries.
2. Not to keep company with men.
3. To be home between the hours of 8:00 p.m. and 6:00 a.m. unless in attendance at a school function.
4. Not to loiter downtown in ice cream stores.
5. Not to leave town at any time without the permission of the chairman of the Board of Trustees.
6. Not to smoke cigarettes. This contract becomes null and void immediately if the teacher is found smoking.
7. Not to drink beer, wine, or whiskey. This contract becomes null and void immediately if the teacher is found drinking beer, wine, or whiskey.
8. Not to ride in a carriage or automobile with any man except her brother or father.
9. Not to dress in bright colors.
10. Not to dye her hair.
11. To wear at last two petticoats.
12. Not to wear dresses more than two inches above the ankles.
13. To keep the schoolroom clean
    a. to sweep the classroom floor at least once daily.
    b. to scrub the classroom floor at least once weekly with hot water and soap.
    c. to clean the blackboard at least once daily.
    d. to start the fire at 7:00 so the room will be warm at 8.00 am. when the children arrive.
14. Not to use face powder, mascara, or paint the lips.

From Apple, M. (1986). *Teachers and Texts*. NY Routledge.

Figure 10. This contract illustrates the rules governing the professional and personal conduct of women teachers in the early 20th century, including restrictions on marriage, social life, dress, and daily duties.[86]

This particular contract is from the early years of the Prohibition Era and five years after the end of World War II. As you can see, the contract has very little to do with actual expectations within the classroom (other than cleaning the classroom and how she presents herself to her students), and more to do with how the teacher represents herself in the community.

Once Prohibition was over, teaching contracts cooled down on temperance and morality (and fear about ice cream stores), focusing more on conventional employment terms, including salary and termination clauses. The contract, however, provides an amusing example of the clear relationship between social trends and norms and what is expected of teachers.

The profession of teaching is not just about teaching; there is a connection between the profession and the social imperatives of the time. "By the 1930s, the dominant paradigm in curriculum is one that was articulated by psychological and social-psychological perspectives."[87]

Women's Right to Vote

Unlike teachers' contracts today, which outline teachers' rights (and are typically negotiated through teachers' unions), in the time of the Industrial Revolution, right after the 19th Amendment was passed—which constitutionally gave women the right to vote for the first time in the United States—some states had already afforded women the right to vote. (The United States has always danced between federal and state authority.) Despite the passing of the amendment, voting was not guaranteed for all women, particularly women of color, who faced continued disenfranchisement through unofficial means such as polling taxes, literacy tests, and voter intimidation. It was not until the Voting Rights Act of 1965 that all women were guaranteed the right to vote.

Desegregation

The Voting Rights Act emerged near the end of the American Civil Rights movement, which began in 1954, the same year as a landmark ruling regarding American public schools. In *Brown v. Board of Education*, the U.S. Supreme Court ruled that state laws establishing separate schools for Black and white children were unconstitutional, overturning the "separate but equal" doctrine established by *Plessy v. Ferguson* in 1896, which effectively segregated students based on race. The ruling was unanimous and is considered by many to be a major milestone in the Civil Rights movement, as it laid the foundation for desegregation efforts in other sectors. Almost a decade later, The Civil Rights Act of 1964 was proposed by President John F. Kennedy in a nationally televised address five months before his assassination and signed into law in July 1964 by President Johnson, after a contentious vote in Congress.[88] The act outlawed discrimination based on race, color, religion, sex, or national origin, addressing a wide array of situations, including public accommodations, libraries, pools, theaters, voting, employment, and any federally assisted programs.

Brown stimulated a series of federal education policies that, in most cases, exist because of tireless advocacy efforts by community members over decades. These policies aimed to give equal access to educational opportunities to children of all backgrounds.

Federal education policies that resulted from *Brown v. Board of Education* by Year

1964: Title IV and Title VI of the Civil Rights Act of 1964 specifically prohibited schools from discriminating on the basis of race, color, or national origin by tying federal funding to compliance. This allowed the federal government to sue schools that resisted desegregation.

1965: The Elementary and Secondary Education Act (ESEA) created a major federal funding program for schools in low-income areas. This aimed to reduce educational inequity by reducing poverty. Title I of the act focused on disadvantaged students.

1968: **The Bilingual Education Act** supported language instruction and services for English Language Learners (ELLs) and was aimed largely at improving educational access for non-English-speaking immigrant children.

1971: ***Swann v. Charlotte-Mecklenburg Board of Education*** allowed busing as a tool for desegregation.

1972: **Title IX of the Educational Amendments to the Civil Rights Act** prohibited gender-based discrimination in federally funded educational institutions. This expanded access to girls and women.

1972: **The Indian Education Act** was the first comprehensive federal law to meet the unique educational needs of Native American students; it provided funding for culturally relevant programs and tribal input. (Note: Native American boarding schools were still in operation.)

1973: **Section 504 of the Rehabilitation Act** was the first civil rights law pertaining to disabilities, mandating accommodations in federally funded schools for students with disabilities.

1974: ***Lau v. Nichols*** ruled that schools must take active steps to help non-English-speaking students access the curriculum. This Supreme Court decision reinforced bilingual education.

1975: **The Indian Self-Determination and Education Assistance Act** allowed tribes to administer their own schools and educational services, moving away from federal assimilationist control.

1975: **The Individuals with Disabilities Education Act (IDEA)** guaranteed free and appropriate public education in the least restrictive environment for children with disabilities.

1982: ***Plyler v. Doe*** guaranteed public education access to undocumented children.

1987: **The McKinney-Vento Homeless Assistance Act** ensured educational access for homeless children and youth.

1990: **The Native American Languages Act** affirmed the right to use and preserve Native languages in education and promoted language revitalization efforts in schools.

Court rulings and federal policies mandating *access* to schools is different from public sentiment, of course; schools were not magically desegregated, workplaces were not immediately nondiscriminatory, and the journey towards racial and ethnic harmony was, and continues to be, complicated. One of the major hurdles was *how* to teach effectively in newly integrated classrooms. The work to create harmony in diversity in American public schools (and, theoretically, flowing outward into American society) has been an ongoing challenge for educators—scholars, educators, families, community leaders—since *Brown v. Board of Education.* Educators developed a number of movements and programs to address the harms caused by assimilationist pedagogies that treated national unity as dependent on erasing cultural difference. These programs sought to affirm the value of diversity in American public schools.

> Of no importance was the fact that the
> Americanization programs were directed,
> only toward people of foreign stock, without
> giving any consideration to the necessity of
> involving all Americans, regardless of the
> time of their arrival in the United States. But,
> above all, the earlier Americanization policies,
> by and large, denied or neglected the strength
> of, and the values in, the foreign culture of
> immigrant groups.[89]
>
> – Leonard Covello, immigrant and longtime New
> York City school teacher and administrator

It is important to remember, as we've been exploring through-out this book, that none of these approaches to education existed in a vacuum or a sealed laboratory! They are informed, shaped, and challenged by social, economic, cultural, and po-litical forces, and shifts within the U.S., and in our relation-ship to the rest of the world. And while they are presented in a somewhat linear progression, they do not represent distinct eras, where one approach ends when the other appears; rather, the order represents when they were first introduced and ap-plied. In fact, an examination of educational practices across the country today would reveal that they all exist today, some-times side by side or in blended form in the same school in different classrooms! This includes contemporary versions of the original assimilationist approaches that formed the original American public school system.

Across all these approaches, it is important to note that youth activism—students speaking out about their own education—has long been a hallmark of American public education. The young Hindu Americans featured in this book are part of that long tradition, using their voices to shape how their communities are represented in the classroom.

Multicultural Education (MCE)

Multicultural education, first theorized by James Bank, emerged in the 1960s and '70s out of the Civil Rights Movement alongside the governmental educational policies listed before. MCE sought to include diverse perspectives in the curriculum, emphasizing tolerance, inclusion, and representation. Banks established five dimensions of MCE:

Content Integration incorporates examples and perspectives from diverse cultures and groups into the curriculum. For example, how might the same historical event have been perceived differently by different groups of Americans?

Knowledge Construction Process helps students understand how knowledge is created and how cultural assumptions, perspectives, and biases shape what is taught. For instance, students might identify whose perspectives are missing in a particular historical description.

Prejudice Reduction fosters students' positive attitudes toward different racial, ethnic, and cultural groups. This includes class activities that seek to reduce stereotypes and increase empathy.

Equity Pedagogy seeks to facilitate academic achievement of students from all backgrounds. This includes teaching approaches such as cooperative learning, scaffolding, and bilingual instruction.

Empowered School and Social Structures rearrange the culture and organization of school so that students across groups experience equality. This includes, for example, examining how students are disciplined and reflects Banks's awareness that schools—and not just classrooms—needed to be transformed.

Banks's vision was bold and powerful, especially when you consider the context within which he first imagined it. MCE focused on the content of the curriculum, making cultures and people that had previously been erased by school more visible in *what* was taught. In practice, however, MCE often results in simply adding "heroes and holidays" lessons to the preexisting curriculum—what educators now refer to as an additive approach. While the goal of MCE is noble, the application frequently amounts to adding diversity sprinkles to an already baked and frosted curricular cake. Nothing foundational shifts in what was being taught, so the implicit message was that "diversity" is a nice addition—but not central—the story of America. That said, this first attempt at recognizing previously erased groups in school raised awareness of the biases and gaps in textbooks, laying the foundation for more generatively disruptive approaches. Other prominent educational scholars, including Sonia Nieto, Christine Sleeter, and Carl A. Grant, made key contributions to expand beyond content inclusion in the 1980s and 1990s. They argued that multicultural education should directly address institutional bias, structural inequality, and power dynamics, warning against tokenism and focusing on teacher education. This laid the groundwork for future pedagogies.

Culturally Relevant Pedagogy (CRP)

The term framework of "culturally relevant pedagogy" was coined by revered educational scholar Gloria Ladson-Billings in her landmark 1995 paper, "Toward a Theory of Culturally Relevant Pedagogy." Based on her ethnographic study of successful teachers of African American students, she defined the CRP framework along three core goals: academic success, cultural competence, and critical consciousness. Ladson-Billings positioned CRP as a response to deficit narratives in education and a call to affirm the identities, histories, and capabilities of marginalized students. It also viewed students' home cultures as assets, not deficits. This was a remarkable shift from assimilation pedagogy. CRP affirms students' cultural identities, shifting the focus from content to pedagogy and student-teacher relationships. This promotes empowerment and social awareness for students.

Scholar Geneva Gay's work expands and deepens Ladson-Billings's research, bridging theory with practice. Focusing on culturally responsive teaching, Gay emphasizes practical classroom strategies, instructional methods, and curriculum design that affirm students' cultures and experiences. Her 1990 book, *Culturally Responsive Teaching: Theory, Research, and Practice*, is foundational in teacher preparation programs and continues to inform teacher education. The core ideas of Gay's book include: culture is central to how students communicate, process information, and relate to the world; teachers must develop cultural knowledge of their students and use it to inform how they teach, what they teach, and how they relate to their students; teaching has affective (relating to emotions) and moral dimensions, and care, connection, and respect are integral to students' academic success.

Culturally Sustaining Pedagogy (CSP)

Culturally Sustaining Pedagogy (CSP) is the most recent incarnation of these educational approaches. Developed in the 2010s as an evolution from Culturally Relevant Pedagogy (CRP), the term was coined by Django Paris. CSP recognizes youth culture, linguistic diversity, and evolving identities and posits that schools should not only recognize the relevance of students' cultural backgrounds in learning but should provide opportunities to *sustain* them. CSP is future-oriented. "Rather than preparing youth to participate in a democracy as it is, CSP seeks to educate youth to imagine and create a democracy as it should be."[90]

CSP sees pluralism as essential to American democracy and views education as a space to protect and nurture cultural pluralism. It validates students' languages and community practices as valuable sources of learning and identity while recognizing that culture is not static and can change over time. CSP engages students as co-creators in shaping schools and society and recognizes transnational identities.

CSP is critiqued for its impracticality, particularly in rigid school systems with limited resources. However, it is still quite new, and the educational landscape is shifting dramatically as I write. We have still to discover the relationship, for instance, between AI and CSP, although some already recognize CSP's significance.

> At the present, one 'right place' for people,
> not AI, is understanding how learning can be
> culturally responsive and culturally sustaining,
> as AI is not even close to being ready to
> connect learning to the unique strengths in a
> student's community and family."
>
> – Dr. Nicole Turner, in a 2023 federal report on
> Artificial Intelligence and the future of teaching
> and learning

We return to the original challenge of American education—How do we weave together social unity while sustaining individual cultures? CSP is often framed as the work of schools and how teachers can affirm students' heritage in the face of assimilationist pressures. But the most enduring work of sustaining a culture often begins at home, long before a child enters a classroom. Revathi, and her daughters Sneha and Sia, show how a family can anchor identity in daily practice while adapting to a changing world.

Revathi, Sia, and Sneha: The Central Processing Unit of a Household

Revathi smiles when she tells me how she compared being Hindu to a Central Processing Unit (CPU) to her older daughter, Sneha, a computer science major. The metaphor clicked instantly:

> If you want, you can decide out of this thing what can be your 10 basic functionalities, and you can probably pick and choose. But you need that core.

> Otherwise tomorrow you say, OK, we don't have to have even one *murti* (a sacred statue of the deity) in our house—one thing is gone. Next, you'll say we don't have to go to the temple—another thing gone. Then, you cannot be Hindu just at a philosophical level. It has to be at a practical level somewhere as well.
>
> Without a CPU, there can be no upgrades and downgrades in the PC. That's the core of a computer to run. So, for you to be a Hindu, you need to have some core values. Smaller things are kind of like add-ons that you can pick and choose ... but you need to have some basic functionalities.

For Revathi, this is not an abstract theory. It's how she runs her household, and it's her answer to the pressures of assimilation that her daughters face every day. "Every household at least should have their own set of ... not rules, but some things that make us Hindu. Then we have to stick to it." She learned this not from lectures but from watching her own mother. "My mom used to do 20 things ... get up every morning and do *puja* (daily act of worship and offering), never eat before doing *puja*, keep chanting while doing *puja*, put a *diya* (light an oil lamp) every evening, do *arathi* (offering of light to the deity). She may not have known how to articulate it, but she did it every day. That's what I tell my daughters—every day, every evening you have to do these things no matter what."

I arrive at Revathi's home just before lunchtime. She greets me at the door with the warmest smile. A delicious aroma already drifting from the kitchen. I am barely seated before she places a plate of *rajma* (red kidney beans) and rice in front of me. It's simple, perfect, and comforting—the kind of welcome that doesn't need explanation. The kind that makes you feel like you belong.

Her daughters, Sneha and Sia, join us soon after, and the energy in the house shifts to more laughter, more teasing, more opinions. We all sit in the living room and talk about school and family, TV shows and campus life, identity and the intensity of growing up both Indian and American. This is not a quiet household. Not because of noise but because of conviction. These are women who speak their minds—sharp, compassionate, and deeply rooted in their values.

Sia, the younger sister, remembers the one-week Hinduism unit she took in sixth grade.

"I had a white teacher, and for all of … when we learned about Christianity, when we learned about Islam, it was very interactive, very … lecture slides and everything," she said. "But then we got to the Hinduism unit, and it was just like, oh, here are the reading pages, take notes. And I was like, oh, cool. We're not going to talk about it."

The contrast stuck with her—not just the brevity but the absence of engagement.

Sneha, now a college graduate, speaks with more distance but just as much clarity. She remembers how Hindu students at her school rarely spoke openly about their faith, while Indian Christian and Indian Muslim peers would freely share about weekend *community* events or religious activities. "Most people are whitewashed Indian people. A lot of them will only say something Hindu or Indian related when it is … in the textbooks … because they were the token brown person to say something. No one was really proud of cultural identity."

Her friends might invite people to a Diwali party but wouldn't say the word "Hindu." She found it disorienting. "If they were Christian, they'd be like, oh, we go to church. One of my best friends … she was so proud of her identity. But none of my other friends would talk about it or even be receptive, which is weird because they were all so Hindu too."

At times, she found it easier to talk about her faith with people of entirely different religions than with fellow Hindus.

> Growing up, there was a big disconnect because
> I'd have all these things that I do at home,
> but I couldn't do them at school. Just small
> things—when a book drops, you do this, touch
> it to your forehead. I wouldn't be embarrassed,
> but I felt like it would be hard explaining to
> other people. I don't have to explain what I'm
> doing—I'm just doing it because that's how I've
> always done it. It's second nature.
>
> – Sneha, on being Hindu at school

That disconnect was sharpened by what she saw in textbooks and classrooms. She would flip ahead before the Hinduism lesson, "just to see what they're going to teach," and found most of it inaccurate. "They have these magnificent churches in the Christianity chapters … and then when you come to the India chapter, everything's super dirty and it looks gross," said Sneha. The first page … some lady who was visibly poor, cleaning trash off the ground. Why is that the first picture?"

Even the tone of instruction felt different.

"They have a basic understanding of the other religions … which they just don't for Hinduism," she said. "Everything they were explaining would be in a very sour undertone. They'd be like 'the monkey god'… weird connotations of everything. So, I'd find myself correcting the teachers so many times because no one else would."

The corrections were met politely in class, but without follow-through. "It was like a save-face type of thing … but it wasn't an actual, genuine effort to learn." For Sneha, the gap between the way other religions were taught—with depth, accuracy, and respect—and the way Hinduism was handled was impossible to miss.

It also shaped what she kept to herself. She loved going to Shakha on Sundays; it was a beautiful part of her week. But she rarely talked about it in school, knowing that anything Hindu was likely to be misunderstood, oversimplified, or ridiculed.

Revathi knows her daughters' experiences aren't unique, and she knows the forces that push Hindu kids toward hiding parts of themselves. "In order to assimilate, they want to let go of the whole Hindu. You cannot be Hindu. Or at most, they'll have a double identity … totally different persona at home and totally different persona with peers. It's not integrated."

For her, the answer is not retreat, but reinforcement. She has no hesitation about being called "regressive," if it means her daughters know exactly who they are and what they stand for. She insists on daily, embodied practices—small, consistent acts that anchor identity in lived reality. "For me at least, sitting in front of God for five, 10 minutes … you are a Hindu. You have to have that connection."

She is clear-eyed about the flexibility of Hindu practice but sees that flexibility as a reason to define one's own household "core," not to let it dissolve. "If everything is so flexible, then there is no definition … So, unless and until you put it down on yourself, there is no way."

The CPU analogy is her way of meeting her daughters where they are.

"At a philosophical level, it's very hard for them … But if you go down to their practical level and tell them, it becomes easier to understand," said Revathi. This is culturally sustaining pedagogy at home—anchoring the basic functionalities of identity while allowing space for the add-ons to change, adapt, and evolve.

As I leave their home, I think about how often we talk about Culturally Sustaining Pedagogy in classrooms—how it's framed as a school-based corrective to assimilationist pressures. But here, in Revathi's living room, between the aroma of rajma and rice and the echo of her daughters' voices debating identity, it's clear that the most enduring work of sustaining culture often happens before a child ever enters a classroom.

CHAPTER FIVE

Hinduism and Hindus in Contemporary American Education

In 1965, the Immigration and Nationality Act (also known as the Hart-Celler Act) transformed American immigration policy, which had previously favored immigrants from Northern and Western Europe while restricting those from other parts of the world. Immigration would now prioritize family reunification and skills-based immigration. With this new policy, U.S. immigrants' country of origin shifted dramatically,[91] sparking debates about the social fabric of the country ... debates that continue to this day.

This means a few things for our story of American public education as it pertains to Hindus.

After India's Independence in 1947, the new Indian government focused largely on re-industrializing the new nation after waves of colonization had de-industrialized the once global power. This required the establishment of engineering and technology schools. The first Indian Institute of Technology was founded in 1950 in Kharagpur, at the site of the Hijli Detention Camp where the British had incarcerated political prisoners.[92] By 1961, four more IITs launched, with financial support and academic cooperation from the USSR, Germany, the U.S., and the UK. In addition, from 1959 onwards, 17 Regional Engineering Colleges (RECs) were established in and funded by state governments. The goal was to not only produce qualified engineers but to create social harmony and a sense of Indian unity by bringing together students from across the states, each speaking different languages with different local traditions.

My father, born in 1942, graduated from the second class of the REC in Warangal; he describes how the physical structure of the college was being erected around them, but also how he was meeting people from across India, from places he had never had the opportunity to visit. (He also describes using a slide rule to study engineering, which my children find endlessly amusing.) There are currently 30 such regional engineering colleges, which are now referred to as National Institutes of Technology.

At the same time that newly independent India was establishing engineering and technology institutes and producing its first batches of engineers and inventors from children who had been born into colonization and were now citizens of the world's largest democracy, the U.S. had officially entered the Space Race and, 10 years later, passed the Hart-Celler Act.

This meant that there was suddenly a surge of Indian immigrants—and, as a matter of proportion of population,

Hindus—who were engineers, technicians, and inventors entering the U.S. to meet the challenges of Kennedy's Moonshot.

The justification for U.S. immigration shifted from "skin" to "skill."[93]

This was the largest migration of Hindus to the U.S. in the nation's history. And they were arriving here because of their training as scientists. During this same period, Hindus from other parts of the world—including East Africa, The Caribbean, Southeast Asia, and the Anglosphere—began entering the country.

For the first time, those "irrational, superstitious heathens" who had been all the way on other side of the globe and had appeared in American geography textbooks as an example of how *not* to be a good American (and whose religion, Americans had been historically taught, was counter to a scientific mind-set) were here ... as scientists contributing to America's big dream, sending their children to our public schools.

From 1960 to 1969, approximately 15,000 Hindus immigrated from India to the U.S. (My father immigrated here in 1966!) Over the decades, the flow increased substantially. In 2023, the Public Religion Research Institute estimated that number of Hindu Americans—which includes immigrants and American-born Hindus—was between 2.7 million and 3.2 million.[94]

Region	1960s	1970s	1980s	1990s	2000s	2010s
India (majority)	15,000	118,000	185,000	282,000	472,000	511,000
East Africa (Kenya, Uganda, Tanzania)	300	2,000	3,000	3,000	5,000	5,000
Caribbean (Guyana, Trinidad & Tobago, Suriname)	300	500	2,000	15,000	35,000	90,000
Southeast Asia (Malaysia, Singapore, Indonesia)	50	100	300	500	700	1,000
Fiji (Indian-Fijian Hindu diaspora)	100	300	500	800	1,200	1,500
UK (Indian-origin Hindu immigrants)	200	300	500	700	1,000	1,500
Canada (Indian-origin Hindu immigrants)	50	100	200	400	800	1,200
Australia (Indian-origin Hindu immigrants)	30	50	100	200	500	800

Figure 11. Hindu Immigration to the U.S. by Region and Decade
* Estimates are based on available immigration data, academic research, and public demographic reports.[95]

Hinduism and Hindus in American Curriculum from the 1960s to the Present

Before we dive into more contemporary representations of Hinduism and Hindus in American schools, I'd like to offer a helpful framework that will help map these trends onto what we first saw in the 19th century.

The Endogenous Cycle of Hinduphobia

An endogenous cycle is a pattern or logic that is self-generating and self-perpetuating. In this case, the cycle has three foundational premises:

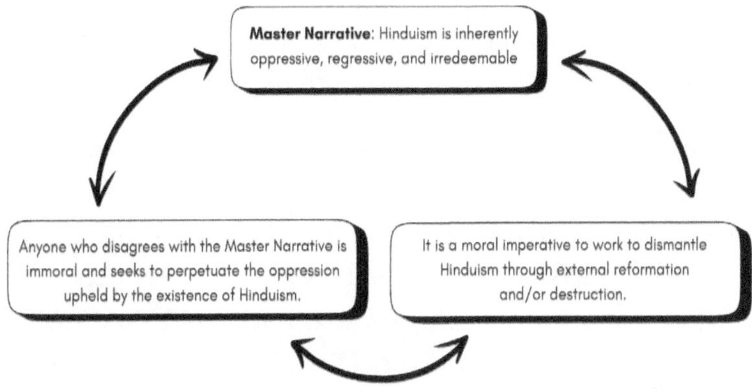

Figure 12. The Endogenous Cycle of Hinduphobia[96]

You should recognize this master narrative from Chapter Two. The old ideas about Hinduism have not changed. Notice that the critique here is not about parts of Hindu society or eras in Hindu history. The critique is that Hinduism itself is inherently terrible and there's nothing that can be done to save it from within. The second premise is that it is a moral priority for outsiders to either take apart Hinduism or erase it entirely. This is an echo of what we read in Chapter Two as well—the American's burden. In this case, there is a call not just to convert Hindus but to completely dismantle the religion. It's taken on some urgency. Finally, the third principle is what keeps the cycle running. No one is allowed to disagree with the Master Narrative or offer another perspective on what Hinduism is; if they do, you should immediately be suspicious of them because they are simply self-preserving oppressors.

It's a case of either you agree with this or you're evil.

Kinda messed up, right? How can something so obviously dishonest sustain—how *has* it sustained for so long?

Three mechanisms sustain the cycle of Hinduphobia: stereotypes, erasure, and testimonial injustice. Stereotypes take a small, often negative fragment of truth, strip it of context, and repeat it so persistently that it becomes the only acceptable version of reality, so much so that any attempt to add nuance or context is treated as a denial of truth. Erasure removes histories, voices, and perspectives (of both Hindu struggles and contributions) from public consciousness and records, until reintroducing them appears revisionist or suspect. Testimonial injustice occurs when Hindus (or any category of people) are presumed unreliable or untrustworthy simply because of who they are, leading their knowledge and experiences to be dismissed before they are even considered.

Now that we've established the mechanisms that sustain the Master Narrative about Hinduism, let's turn our attention back to schools and textbooks. In Chapter One, we looked at how geography textbooks used in the Common School Era portrayed Hindus and Hinduism. At that time, geography served as the primary portal through which American teachers helped students understand their national identity and their place in the world. Over time, geography evolved into the broader field of social studies, encompassing history, geography, civics and government, economics, culture and society, anthropology, psychology, sociology, global studies, and contemporary world issues.

Let's now bring these two threads together—the endogenous cycle and social studies—to examine how Hinduism has been represented in American schools since Hindus first arrived in the U.S. To do this, we'll turn to educational scholar Yvette Rosser's survey of K–12 curricula across the decades and distill the key themes that emerge.

1960s through 1980s: Erasure and Oversimplification in Early Curriculum

During this period, Rosser observes that "Hinduism is included among the 'World's Five Great Religions' and yet paradoxically, Hindu beliefs and traditions are often represented as a localized collection of complex archaic cults, characterized quintessentially by the evil caste system."[97]

Education publishers like Holt McDougal and Houghton Mifflin produce textbooks where Hinduism is either excluded completely or is presented as an archaic, strange "world religion." The presence of Hindus in the U.S. is completely erased. The Hinduism of these textbooks is disconnected from real, relatable people or practices. Depicted in the context of India as a poor and stagnant country, Hinduism is reduced to ritual obsession, oppressiveness, polytheism, and a kind of irrationality and incoherence.

1980s to 1990: Stereotyping and Selective Inclusion

As we discussed in the previous chapter, multicultural education is taken up widely in American education during this era. While it may be well-intentioned, it can remain tokenist. (Remember the sprinkles?) Indeed, this is how Hinduism appears in school textbooks during this period. Rosser notes that festivals are represented in surface-level ways (i.e., without an explanation of their deeper significance), and there remains a fixation on sensationalist descriptions of Hinduism's multiple gods and the caste system. She also notes that the imagery and terminology is still very exoticizing and othering of Hindu practices. Hindus are strange people doing strange things in a strange country on the other side of the world. Old stereotypes continue to be reinforced, as if the only thing that is true and worth knowing about Hinduism are that cows are sacred, caste oppression is foundational, and women are oppressed through practices like *sati*, or widow immolation. No context is given for any of this, including historical or scriptural.

1990s to Present: Hinduism is Casteism

In a 2001 article, "The Clandestine Curriculum: The Temple of Doom in the Classroom,"[98] published in the journal *Education About Asia*, Rosser unpacks the hidden Hinduism curriculum within American classrooms. The article offers a methodical breakdown of how standards, textbooks, and methods of teaching enliven the old stereotypes and caricatures we've been discussing throughout this book. I highly recommend reading the piece in its entirety, but here is one important excerpt:

If being born in a certain caste is by chance, like the drawing of lots, then it is certainly cavalier and unfair. But, if the caste system is explained in the context of the broader epistemology, including a discussion of Dharma (duty, personal spiritual path) and karma, then the original concept—dividing the work of society up according to the skill and predilection of the individual—does not seem inherently evil but has a rationale, which is seldom explained to school children.

The caste system, as taught in American classrooms, is represented as the exact opposite of our democratic institutions. If a rigid caste system is employed to explain the primary expression or essence of Indic civilization, it makes that culture seem heartless and quite unfair and does not further the understanding of the fluidity and mobility inherent in Hinduism. This critique is not offered as an apology for the caste system, but as an alternative to negatively objectifying caste as the evil other that ultimately becomes the hallmark of Indian civilization. In a survey of high school level world history textbooks, I found that more space is devoted to the caste system than all the other characteristics of Hindu India combined, such as art, literature, architecture, philosophy, economics, politics, and the culturally rich and diverse population.

In textbooks, few other aspects of Hinduism are considered as relevant or dealt with in comparable depth as is the caste system. What is downplayed or rarely mentioned are India's post-independence efforts toward national integration of its minorities and low caste citizens.

An audit of currently used textbooks reveals troubling inaccuracies, clear misrepresentations, and strange depictions and absences.

The Origins of Our Discontents

Isabel Wilkerson's popular book, *Caste: The Origins of Our Discontents*, is partially based on "observations" she conducted in India within communities that don't speak English. She does not speak their languages. **And she didn't use a translator.**

Yoga

Yoga is a helpful example. It is rarely given the attention it deserves when teaching about Hinduism, despite the fact that it provides a very accessible and relatable entry point into illuminating Hindu principles, practices, and philosophies. States like Texas avoid mention of yoga altogether in schools. When it is represented, it is reduced to physical postures and referenced as a cultural practice in South Asia.

For instance, Education publisher Savvas produces curricular materials, including textbooks, that are widely approved for use across California. In Savvas's *myWorld Interactive: Ancient*

Civilizations, Grade 6 (California edition) textbook it states, "Some Hindus practice yoga, a series of physical and mental exercises to aid meditation." This suggests a surface-level connection between yoga and Hinduism, and a reductive representation of yoga, itself. The History-Social Science (HSS) Framework for California Public Schools (2016) asserts, "Students learn that Hindu beliefs and practices, including yoga, spread beyond India and have influenced cultures throughout Asia and the world." This is somewhat more than Savvas's representation … but is it really? Are we really getting much information about the deeper framework of yoga? Yoga is an "influence" on cultures, not a larger framework toward self-knowledge. There is no mention of the five *Yamas* (social ethics): *Ahimsa* (non-violence), *Satya* (truthfulness), *Asteya* (non-accumulation), *Brahmacharya* (moderation or conservation of energy), and *Aparigraha* (non-attachment); or the *Niyamas* (ethical observances): *Soucha* (internal and external cleanliness), *Santosha* (contentment), *Tapas* (austerity), *Swadhyaya* (self-study) and *Ishvarapranidhana* (surrender to the higher power).

As Rosser notes, Hinduism is often "presented without reference to its internal coherence." By contrast, California school curricula incorporate the embodied practices of Christianity, Islam, and Judaism, and are situated along with their greater spiritual significance, including devotion, morality, and reverence.

The California HSS Framework includes explicit references to Christian practices such as baptism, Holy Communion, and the significance of Jesus's resurrection. These are explained with doctrinal clarity and without skepticism. Christian holidays like Christmas and Easter are described as religious and cultural traditions in a celebratory tone.

Islamic embodied practices are routinely included and described with attention to meaning and observance. The Savvas 6th grade textbook includes sections on the Five Pillars of Islam, specifically *Sala* (prayer), *Sawm* (fasting during Ramadan), and *Hajj* (pilgrimage to Mecca) with a tone of respectful explanation. Visual depictions often include Muslims in prayer, and terminology like "submission to God" is clarified with care.

Jewish rituals and embodied practices such as observing Shabbat, *kashrut* (keeping kosher), and celebrating a Bar/Bat Mitzvah are typically presented with cultural and religious reverence. In California textbooks and frameworks, Judaism is described with reference to core religious practices and holidays (e.g., Passover, Yom Kippur), and the Ten Commandments are highlighted as foundational moral teachings.

School isn't just about textbooks and standards.

There are three dominant ideas that circulate in conversations about yoga in schools in the U.S. The first is that Yoga is devil worship and has no place in our public schools. This reflects the oldest and most overtly anti-Indigenous, Hinduphobic narrative about yoga. The second idea is that yoga is for everyone. This concept—imported from the Yoga Industrial Complex, or the commercialization of yoga, opens the door for anyone to teach and learn "secularized" yoga in schools. The third idea, which stitches together social justice narratives from the Yoga Industrial Complex with critical analysis in education, critiques yoga (and meditation) that is taught in schools as discriminatory and oppressive. Each of these ideas layer atop the previous one, enacting the language of social justice while demonizing and/or delegitimizing the Hindu tradition.

These are not new ideas.

Figure 13. "Mysterious Yoga Faith of East India Which Has Robbed an American Citizen of a Devoted Wife," *The Washington Times* (1908).

What is the end result of such a curriculum? What is the mythology being taught to all American students—and therefore, all of American society—about Hinduism, as a tradition? The same mythology that has been taught for hundreds of years, beginning with the Common Schools and now baked into the American public school system?

Yoga has long been narrated in the U.S. as a dangerous path towards barbarism and Heathenism, stealing, in particular, innocent American women. According to an article from *The Washington Times* on the topic from 1908 about a wife who took yoga, "And she accepted, in the place of all this, a life of semi-barbarity, among the mystics, the fakers, and the dervishes of East India, where as a devotee of the weird, intangible faith which is called Yoga, she must satisfy her heart's desire in the contemplation of the occult."

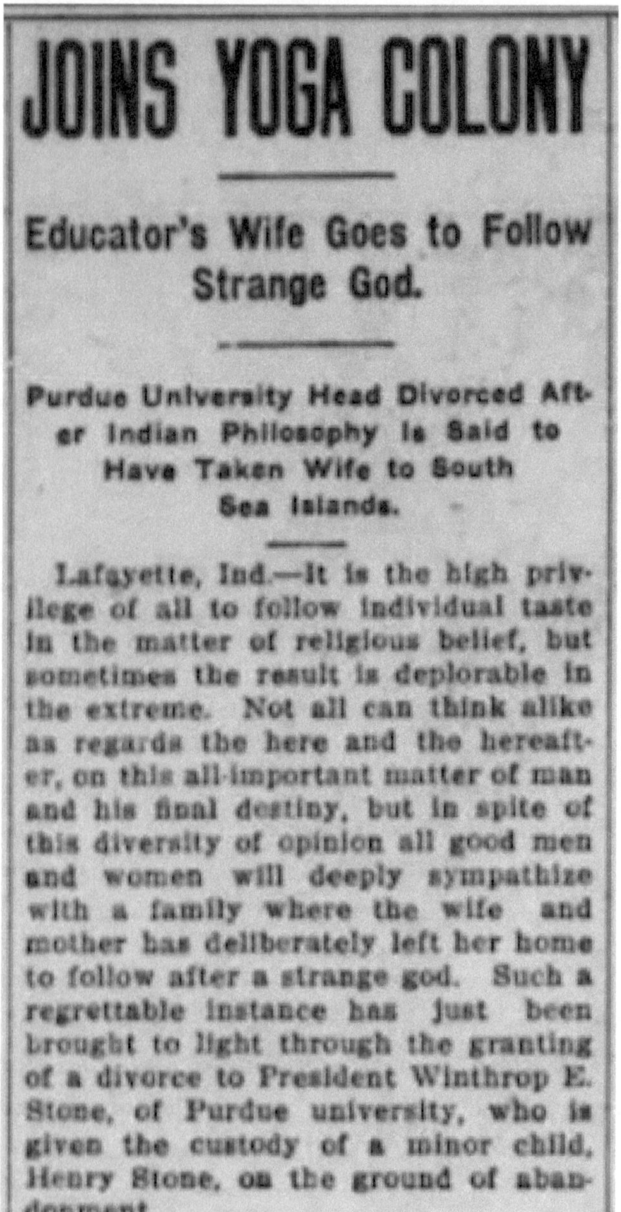

JOINS YOGA COLONY

Educator's Wife Goes to Follow Strange God.

Purdue University Head Divorced After Indian Philosophy Is Said to Have Taken Wife to South Sea Islands.

Lafayette, Ind.—It is the high privilege of all to follow individual taste in the matter of religious belief, but sometimes the result is deplorable in the extreme. Not all can think alike as regards the here and the hereafter, on this all-important matter of man and his final destiny, but in spite of this diversity of opinion all good men and women will deeply sympathize with a family where the wife and mother has deliberately left her home to follow after a strange god. Such a regrettable instance has just been brought to light through the granting of a divorce to President Winthrop E. Stone, of Purdue university, who is given the custody of a minor child, Henry Stone, on the ground of abandonment.

Figure 14. "Joins Yoga Colony: Educator's Wife Goes to Follow Strange God," *Charlevoix County Herald,* East Jordan, Michigan (1911).

College campuses were particularly vulnerable. A 1911 article from the *Charlevoix County Herald* declared, "Joins Yoga Colony: Educator's Wife Goes to Follow Strange God." The article warns that a Mrs. Stone's entrapment in this cult led her to abandon her husband and child. "It was taught that a complete fulfillment of 'Yoga philosophy' involved the separation from family, friends, and kindred, Mrs. Stone became a devout follower of the faith and left home ... in this island where Mrs. Stone is supposed to be its members are called sun worshippers."

The common thread throughout these warnings is that yoga will lead innocent Americans away from their Christian God and values. Yoga's strange god steals wives, leaves children motherless ... and leads to divorce.

One hundred years later, in 2012, we see the contemporary version of this through the protest against yoga in schools. A *Seattle Times* article from November reports that "Encinitas School District officials never thought yoga, practiced by roughly 22 million Americans, would be controversial when they accepted a $533,000 grant from a local yoga studio to include Ashtanga yoga in a program." The article leans into the pun, describing how parents "are in a twist over yoga, saying that adding the ancient practice of meditative exercise to the school curriculum is tantamount to religious indoctrination into Hinduism." The chief executive of the yoga studio, in response to the protest, responded, "It's hard to know how to respond to someone who says if you touch your toes, you're inviting the devil into your soul."

Various debates go back and forth about whether or not yoga should be banned in schools (because it is Hindu and therefore anti-Christian) or allowed (because it is "secular" and has no connection to a religion). Rarely are Hindus included in these conversations and debates.

In a 2018 article in *The Atlantic*, journalist Alia Wong clarifies that school-based yoga focuses on physical exercises, relaxation, and mindfulness, including exercise breaks kids take at their desks. Marlynn Wei, a "certified yoga teacher" claims that by quote "removing yoga's more superficial aspects (such as Sanskrit words and symbols), yoga can still have mindfulness and be appreciated for its benefits beyond physical exercise.

She goes on to classify yoga-based lesson plans, teacher trainings and mindfulness playlists on the internet as a part of school-based yoga, as well as certified yoga instructors who want to bring their practice to schools. New York University psychologist Bethany Butzer identified 36 programs reaching 940 schools with more than 5,400 instructors:

> In reality, school-based yoga typically focuses on physical exercise or on relaxation and mindfulness. Some schools integrate it via in-classroom lessons that have kids engage in a few exercises at their desk during short breaks throughout the day. Other schools adopt yoga as an in- or after-school elective, while some incorporate it into regular PE classes.

> "Many original forms of yoga are practiced in a religious or spiritual manner," acknowledges Marlynn Wei, a psychiatrist, therapist, and certified yoga teacher who's written about yoga's educational uses. Still, religion-infused yoga often pursues the same ends as its secular counterpart: For example, they both emphasize being in the

present. By removing yoga's more superficial aspects (such as Sanskrit words and symbols), yoga can still have mindfulness and be appreciated for its benefits beyond physical exercise, Wei says.

Not only are folks determining what qualifies as yoga, they are also determining what is feasible to implement, and who is a qualified quote-unquote "yoga instructor."

(Now I want to make a point here that I'm very sympathetic to the teaching force. They've been told they have a right and freedom to do this by certified yoga experts and people with doctorates. Every message coming from the Yoga Industrial Complex tells them this is perfectly alright. What's really insidious here is that schoolteachers are fatigued and burned out and still want to care for their students. They're underpaid and they are not necessarily making a profit off teaching this to their students. This kind of business takes advantage of their sincerity, leads to burn out, and frustration with a system that places far too much on their shoulders.)

Yoga in schools very quickly gets reduced to social emotional learning, exercise … "wellness." Anyone can make up anything they want and call it yoga. "Yoga" is separated from its source tradition, and defined as postures and breathing by schools, journalists, psychologists, and judges. It is taught through YouTube videos or by teachers trained without context of the philosophical framework of yoga or requirements to have a personal practice (which is how yoga works!).

Guess what happens next?

Are you sitting?

Yoga is now called "biopolitics," according to University of Hong Kong Education Professor Liz Jackson. In her article "Must Children Sit Still? The Dark Biopolitics of Mindfulness and Yoga in Education," that appeared in the journal *Educational Philosophy and Theory* in 2020, she writes:

> That yoga is particularly recommended for dealing with "problem" children, "urban youth," and those diagnosed with disabilities and disorders is noteworthy in this context. Socially deprived children are often labelled in discourses of self-care as vulnerable to mental and emotional difficulties, as if the vulnerability has nothing to do with social deprivation. The vulnerability, dislocated from its true cause, is then treated as something that children should be accountable for, and as something that they should learn that they are accountable for. In this context, focusing on yoga serves to distract from focusing on injustice, among educators and students. In the case of programmes oriented toward "urban youth" in the United States, it is also important to question how desire to control black bodies functions beneath the surface of benevolent discourse ascribing to yoga practice socially transformative means (Andrews, 2013). Why exactly must children sit still, and lie on the ground in the yoga "corpse" pose, in classrooms? Who most clearly benefits here? Additionally, victim-blaming approaches teach hidden lessons, as students learn to see themselves as problem children, whose attitudes are apparently the cause of the challenges they face.

Jackson notes that yoga is prescribed as an intervention to deal with "problem children, urban youth, and those diagnosed with disabilities and disorders." Educational research has long and fastidiously documented that students of color are disproportionately placed into each of these categories. She continues "it is also important to question how desire to control black bodies functions beneath the surface of benevolent discourse ascribing to yoga practice socially transformative means. Why exactly must children sit still and lie on the ground in the yoga "corpse" pose. Victim-blaming approaches teach hidden lessons, as students learn to see themselves as problem children, whose attitudes are apparently the cause of the challenges they face."

Cleaved from the source tradition, philosophies and meanings, this empty ghost of "yoga" has been introduced into complex, troubling school spaces so that the issues and tensions and power dynamics that exist in schools are mapped onto yoga itself. While yoga is meant to be a part of a seeker's spiritual journey, it is now mandatory exercise to manage behavior. The significance of Shavasana has been twisted into an attack on children of color!

Wait … there's more!

In February of 2021, the *The News Journal* (Delaware)[99] reported that an early childhood teacher asked her students to re-enact the journey of enslaved Africans over the Atlantic using yoga poses. Remember, role-play has an incredibly influential impact on the mind:

> The Caesar Rodney School District is investigating a Black History Month lesson that some parents are calling "culturally insensitive, offensive" and "disturbing."

The prerecorded hybrid lesson was taught at the Mcllvaine Early Childhood Center. A short clip shared by a parent on Facebook shows part of the 35-minute class, where a teacher combines yoga poses with her version of how Africans were enslaved and brought to America.

"African people came to America on boats to become slaves," the teacher says in the video. "So here's the great big country of Africa. They crossed the Atlantic to come over to America. So right now, I need you to get into your boat pose," she says, demonstrating the yoga pose.

"Came? We were stolen," the mother recording the video is heard saying.

It's incredibly important to note, here, that the journalist makes no attempt to separate the teacher's horrifying lesson from yoga. Apart from the centuries of colonization and enslavement in India, Hindus were also stolen and enslaved and brought to the West Indies.

In just a few sentences, the history of Hindus and the meaning of yoga is erased. In their place, yoga is now associated with a horrifying, traumatic whitewashed lesson on enslavement.

Now, yoga itself is "oppressive."

Most Hindu immigrant parents are appalled when they understand that this is explicitly and implicitly being taught to our children through the public school system. Hindu American parents like me, who grew up in the U.S., are familiar with the misrepresentation and caricaturization of Hinduism. But we also grew up in the '70s, '80s, and '90s, when the depictions of Hinduism in school were caricaturized, reductive, and exoticized. Classrooms didn't have the same charge they do now. That charge has been magnified by social media and changes in the sociopolitical landscape.

So, what is the final message from all of this? The perpetuation of a kind of mythology *about* Hinduism that has been enlivened and carried on in American schools for nearly two centuries:

The most important thing to remember about Hinduism is casteism, which is the same as racism:

Hinduism is inherently, theologically oppressive and backward.

Hinduism is an incoherent set of strange practices and beliefs.

Hindus have not done anything to correct inequity and harm within Hindu/Indian society.

If someone in the U.S. practices Hinduism, they are inherently "casteist" because it is integral to their religion.

Hindus—including Hindu Americans—are to be suspected. Their faith teaches them to be oppressive.

It is a humanitarian imperative to eradicate or correct oppression in the world, including Hinduism.

Hinduism is incompatible with democracy.

Even in the most formal arenas of public education, the stories told about Hinduism can feel unmoored from how it is actually understood and lived. In one Bay Area family, that gap was met with preparation. A mother's steadfast instruction in

Dharma, democracy, and self-respect shaped children ready to speak for themselves. What followed was a moment when a seventh-grader's words made the official record, and the prevailing narrative suddenly seemed harder to defend.

Vayu and Divya: The Dinosaur Argument

Vayu, a rising college senior, leans back, speaking with clarity and wit, sharing reflections that bounce between the deeply personal and the sharply political. We are sitting outside a Starbucks, the sun casting long shadows as the morning drifts toward noon. A few days earlier, I sat with his mother, Divya, in the warmth of her living room. She had graciously hosted me in California—sharing food, space, stories. There's something grounding about the quiet care with which she welcomes me and something electric in the passion that Vayu brings.

> Does that mean dinosaurs didn't
> exist before paleontologists came
> up with the word "dinosaur"?
>
> – Vayu

Vayu was in eighth grade when he delivered that line before the California Department of Education in 2016. The hearing room was full. State officials, educators, parents, and students gathered to weigh in on revisions to the social studies framework. On one side, a group of South Asian scholars argued that the word "India" should be removed from textbooks, claiming that the nation of India did not exist before 1947. On the other, a coalition of parents, students, and community members—Hindu and otherwise—insisted that erasing the name was historically inaccurate and damaging.

For Vayu, the argument about terminology was not just an abstract debate; it was about logic, about whether labels determine existence. "Just because the name 'India' was formally used later doesn't mean the land, the civilizations, the people didn't exist," he said. "Same with Hinduism. It's had many different names over time. That doesn't make it less real."

His dinosaur analogy landed because it was disarming—funny, even—but also precise.

Vayu is planning to become a defense attorney. He laughed about the nerves he'd felt that day. "I never really spoke before. I spoke a few times at some public speaking things, but I was a little nervous, don't get me wrong. My main thing was I wanted to speak because I never really had an experience in public speaking. I saw my peers doing it. I saw their parents doing it. My parents were definitely speaking, so I didn't want to feel left out. I want to say something as well. My voice should matter as equally as everyone else's."

He knew his contribution would echo others' points. "But I didn't want to be left out. I wanted to say something as well. My voice should matter as equally as everyone else's."

The day wasn't without hostility. "They called us Nazis, fascists … which is, first of all, an insult to millions of Jews and millions of other people who were killed by the Nazis," he said. "And also they're just taking this term and muddling it down because we just want to protect our beliefs. We want people to know about us in a true, unbiased way, and they want to change that." Vayu remembers one woman yelling at him, calling him names. "I was in eighth grade," he said. The tone, he says, was less about debate and more about demeaning.

Before meeting Vayu, I had stayed with his mother, Divya, during the first part of my Bay Area research trip. Her home was a place of constant welcome—meals that seemed to appear out of nowhere, tea refilled without asking, conversation that moved easily between the serious and the lighthearted. Her warmth as a hostess was matched by a clarity of purpose when she spoke about why she and her children participated in the hearings.

She arrived in New York not long after the Dotbusters' hate group attacks of the 1980s, when Hindus were warned not to appear visibly Hindu in public. She had no intention of passing on that fear to her children.

> We as Hindus don't have such extreme feelings
> about anything, that we are moderate by
> nature, by religion. We are democratic and we
> are moderate thinkers. My idea was to make
> my children understand that life is about being
> a moderate thinker, about being democratic,
> and that no kind of authoritarianism should
> affect our growing up.
>
> – Divya on setting an example for her children

For her daughter, Amrita, that meant an unspoken education about gender. "We like to say that India is patriarchal ... but to even think that this is not a patriarchal society is so far away from the truth," said Vayu. "Without telling my daughter that we are in a patriarchal world, I wanted to make sure she understands how one needs to be as a woman."

Divya has also seen how new immigrants hesitate to speak. "They do not know if they can talk for themselves," she said. "They're afraid … will they be deported? So, these fears exist in the new immigrants. We don't have those issues because we are citizens of this country and our children are citizens of this country. So, the idea for me was to make sure that more second-generation citizens of this country actually learn how to fight … and pass the torch through them."

At the hearings, she and other organizers brought food for everyone, regardless of which "side" they were on. "Our kids would go to the vending machine and they would … say, 'Auntie, I saw that lady there in the bathroom and she was making sure she didn't see me,'" she said. "One of the things that I think the opposing team could not do was look us in the eye. They couldn't even see our children. They didn't have any children coming. They couldn't see."

What struck her most was the refusal to engage with the students as individuals. "They just decided for us, they judged us … Without even thinking, 'Let us ask the child, did your mother write this for you? Did your father write this for you?' Nobody did. Again, they just decided."

Vayu's own testimony showed the results of her approach. His reasoning was both grounded in history and attuned to analogy, able to connect a textbook terminology dispute to something universally understood. He has a habit of talking through ideas in layers, mapping them across contexts.

Hinduism and Americanism … They work
together very well. Because like Hinduism,
you can't paint America with a single brush.
It's not one concrete country with one
concrete political system, political beliefs.
If anything, you've got 50 states plus all the
legal jurisdictions … We're all in different
small countries but federated as one. And
under the auspices that out of many, we are
one. I'd say Hinduism is a lot like that too.
We have many, many different beliefs … but
we all believe in the same basic tenets.

– Vayu on how Hinduism and
Americanism are complementary

He sees Hinduism not as a monolith but as a federation of
approaches, much like the U.S. That analogy—unexpected
yet apt—echoes the same instinct that fueled his "dinosaur"
remark: Start from something relatable, then show how it illuminates the more complex whole.

When I think back to my time with Vayu in the noisy comfort
of a Starbucks and talking with Divya in the calm of her living
room, I see two halves of the same commitment. One is the willingness to stand up and speak, even when it's uncomfortable or
when the argument has been made before. The other is the belief
that the next generation should inherit not just the freedom to
speak, but the tools, confidence, and grounding to do it well.

In their family, inquiry is not a performance for outsiders; it
is an internal habit, honed over years, that makes public engagement possible. Divya's kitchen-table conversations about

democracy and moderation are as much a part of Vayu's public voice as his own study of history or law. And in a hearing room where erasure and stereotyping threatened to flatten a tradition, a teenager's joke about dinosaurs managed to widen the frame—reminding everyone that existence doesn't wait for permission to be named.

CHAPTER SIX

Public Pedagogy and the Export of American Education: "Hinduism is the Enemy of Democracy!"

> Whatever Hindus may say, actually, it does not make a difference (to the fact) that Hinduism is a danger to independence, equality, and brotherhood. Thus, it is the enemy of democracy.

When and where do you think this was said? Who might have said it? In what context? If you've made it this far in the book, the premise of this bold statement shouldn't be too shocking. We've already covered how these ideas have been embedded in American public education since its birth. Perhaps it is a statement from back then! Or maybe a politician, worried about the sudden influx of Hindus in the middle of the 20th century, who wrote an essay, warning their fellow Americans about the dangers of Hindus arriving on American shores.

The truth might surprise you.

This statement was made during a 2021 virtual conference titled "Dismantling Global Hindutva." It was made by P. Sivakami, a writer and former officer of the Indian Administrative Service, the country's highest-ranking civil service corps. While the conference was held online, it was oriented toward American scholars, professors, activists, and journalists and reportedly had more than 10,000 registrants. This was not a small gathering.

Nor was Sivakami's message about Hinduism (not "Hindutva") unique. In fact, the three-day conference was filled with similar statements about the inherent danger of Hinduism, with some speakers declaring that Hinduism itself is what needs to be dismantled for democracy to thrive, and that any Hindu who argued otherwise was to be distrusted. This inspired me to write the Endogenous Cycle paper and motivated a collective of Hindu American organizations to write an open letter to America.

To contextualize this, the conference was sponsored by more than 60 prestigious American universities—the who's who of *The U.S. News & World Report's* college rankings.

Naturally, this concerned many members of the Hindu American community, especially the parents of college students who attend these very universities. They wrote to the sponsoring schools out of concern that these statements and impressions would create an actively hostile environment for their children on campus. They asked for additional perspectives to be included by campuses to provide viewpoint diversity. (These letters are publicly available.)

In response, thousands of scholars signed a declaration in support of the conference and its claims: Hindu Americans were accused of trying to stifle American democracy.

The conference organizers, speakers, and their supporters claimed that *they* were victims of a powerful and nefarious global network of Hindus seeking to destroy free speech. It is irrational to argue that they are speaking "truth to power" when they are the gatekeepers of some of the most elite, moneyed, powerful academic institutions in the world. Thirty-five percent of the total signatures in support of the conference and its claims came from 25 federally funded American institutions of higher learning. (Remember back to those federal education policies that emerged from the Civil Rights Act?)

Even if you can explain how this came to be supported by so many elite American universities, how do you explain why Hindus from India were making these claims during the conference? In fact, why do you find so many young, progressive Hindus from India making somewhat similar claims—on social media, in news media, in entertainment media, and in American universities?

There are several factors at play, but there are two mechanisms that have emerged from American education that help contextualize this phenomenon.

The Export of American K-12 Education

The U.S., as we discussed earlier, has and continues to produce and incubate rich, effective ways of educating our youth. Not only is it a reflective discipline—reviewing, reassessing, and reimagining its role and purpose and how to carry it out—but it is incredibly thoughtful. K-12 classrooms are sites of innovation and explore modalities of teaching that go far beyond content delivery.

It can be helpful to think about this in the context of the following teaching categories:

Transmission Models (teacher centered) – The idea is that the teacher holds all the knowledge and actively delivers the content to the students who don't have the knowledge and passively receive it. Direct instruction was one such model, where teachers delivered tightly scripted lectures to students. Behaviorism was another model, shaping learning through repetition and reinforcement of desired behaviors.

Constructivist Models (student centered) – Students construct knowledge by actively participating in the learning process. Project-based learning, inspired by John Dewey and William Heard Kilpatrick, emerged in the early 1900s–1920s. Students work on extended, real-world projects that integrate multiple subjects. Piagetian constructivist approaches, designed around students' stages of cognitive development, significantly influenced elementary schools from the 1950s onward. Vygotskian social constructivism posits that learning happens through social interaction and guided support within a learner's potential range. Inquiry-based learning, with roots in Dewey's progressivism from the early 20th century, became a staple in science education reforms post-Sputnik. Here, students investigate questions or problems to construct new knowledge.

Experiential and Progressive Pedagogies – These models connect classroom learning with "real life" outside the classroom. They were first inspired by Dewey's idea that education grounded in real life relevance helps prepare active citizens. Service learning combines community service with structured reflection to connect learning and civic responsibility. In the Montessori method (designed by Italian physician and educator Maria Montessori, who, interestingly, studied Indigenous Indian models of teaching and learning), children direct their own learning in a prepared environment with hands-on materials.

Critical and Transformative Pedagogies – Critical pedagogies examine how institutions of power influence what is taught and why and aim to create critical thinkers. (We discussed some examples of transformative pedagogies, like culturally relevant pedagogy and culturally sustaining pedagogy, a few chapters ago.)

Skills and Competency-based Models – These emergent models, born in the 21st century, measure student progress through their mastery of defined skills, not by time in the classroom. This approach also includes hybrid (online and in person) teaching models as well as applied STEAM/STEM education.

These approaches to teaching and learning, including the ways in which American education frames and thinks about things like culture and citizenship development (as we've been discussing throughout), are researched and shared with folks from around the world through American schools of education and educational conferences, both of which welcome foreign participants, including Indian educators. And, as a result and as are all things American, these ways of teaching and educating are often exported from the U.S. to the rest of the world, which can be very … complicated.

If we've seen anything over the course of this book, it is that K-12 education is a deeply *situated* practice; it reflects local histories, cultures, conflicts and struggles. Education is not a neutral technology that can simply be extracted from its country of origin and crop dusted across other countries. In fact, even within the U.S., there is so much regional and local diversity that it wouldn't make sense to universalize pedagogies.

Yet, the ways in which American K-12 educational discourse imagines India and Hinduism, and the ways in which that imagined India and Hinduism are critiqued through some of these more critical approaches to teaching, is precisely how some Indian education scholars and educators imagine and critique India and Hinduism. Because there is a permission structure to do so. This is not at all to suggest that the Indian educational system has been taken over by American education. But it is worthwhile to examine the discourses and practices of the progressive educations of the Indian elite and the Indian educational projects that are funded by American dollars.

Unfortunately, formal education is not the only way that American educational concepts about Hinduism and Hindus reach Indians shores. There is also public pedagogy.

What is public pedagogy?

Public pedagogy refers to how public-facing media—entertainment, journalism, social media—teach the public about something. In other words, this is a kind of teaching and learning that happens outside of formal educational institutions. Think of all the kids who "learn" about current events on TikTok. Or think about all the Americans who learn about various medications through television advertisements and then, armed with this new "expertise," demand these treatments from their physicians.

Not all public pedagogy explicitly teaches. Think about the hidden curriculum in the media that normalizes biases, stereotypes, and disinformation. *Indiana Jones and the Temple of Doom* is the one that comes to mind from my own childhood: Dr. Jones is the hero and the monkey-brain eating devil worshippers are the villains. It's pretty clear which side the film wants you to think is the right one. Less explicit examples of public pedagogy include throwaway comments on television shows about how "gooroos" are cult leaders and people who practice yoga are irrational or unintelligent. They rarely do anything to advance the storyline, yet they pervade American entertainment, which is consumed and internalized by a global audience.

Not all public pedagogy is negative! Public service announcements about the dangers of forest fires, for instance, or the need to turn off the tap to conserve water while brushing your teeth resulted in a growth of ecological safety and environmental responsibility across American communities. *Mister Rogers' Neighborhood* is one of my favorite examples of public pedagogy. From 1968 to 2001, Fred Rogers taught young children the values of compassion, kindness, emotional honesty, imagination, curiosity, nonviolence, peace, and community responsibility.

These examples might lead you to believe that public pedagogy is a relatively newer phenomenon—perhaps a byproduct of the television era or the digital age. But it's actually quite old! Remember all those newspaper clippings about the dangers of yoga? That was 19th-century public pedagogy!

In fact, newspapers and magazines were a popular mechanism of public pedagogy during that time.

Figure 15. Cartoon from *Harper's Weekly* (September 30, 1871).

Thomas Nast, a famous political satirist for *Harper's Weekly*, was often described as the Father of the Political Cartoon. He is most popularly known for targeting the corrupt New York City political machine led by Boss Tweed and Tammany Hall. In the image above, Nast captured the popular representations of the "Hindoo religion" from schools and magazines in the cartoon, "The American River Ganges." Hindus carry deep reverence for Ganga (the Ganges), which is one of our holy rivers.

"Drawing on the image of children sacrificed to the Ganges River popularized in missionary reports and schoolbook accounts of Hindoo superstition, Nast pivoted from Hindoo superstition to Catholic superstition. A Protestant pastor with a Bible in his coat protected the children from Catholic crocodiles crawling out of the river. The Vatican rose in the background, while on the right side the US public school crumbled."[100]

Thomas Nast used Hinduism as a foil, a caricature of the dangers of Catholicism, to establish the necessity of Protestant morality as the foundation of American culture.

Today's public pedagogy about Hinduism is more digital and the language and imagery reflect contemporary contexts. Often, it is much more subtly encoded. It can be baked into how stories are told and who the "good guys" and "bad guys" are (spoiler alert: Hindus) in the majority of shows on Amazon Prime India. One of the lessons remains largely the same—Hindus and Hinduism are to be feared. They are immoral, regressive, oppressive, and counter to the values and priorities of democracy and progressive society.

Another, more recent form of public pedagogy is diversity training and workshops in professional and community settings. While these can be helpful approaches to nourish intergroup communication and empathy and reduce harm, they can also have an adverse effect, if we don't take the time to examine their outcomes and implications.

I was fortunate to be on the research team on a study conducted by the Social Perceptions Lab,[101] which examined the effects of diversity training rhetoric on *perceptions* of discrimination. The study was designed as an experiment. In the first part, participants read one of three "priming" passages and were presented with a hypothetical scenario. They then answered questions about the scenario. The limb of the study for which I was a content expert focused on the impact of anti-caste discrimination trainings on perceptions of caste discrimination in the U.S. One-third of participants (we'll call them Group A) were presented with a passage that was extracted from Equality Labs' literature, perhaps the loudest American organization offering workshops on the issue of American caste-based discrimination. (Equality Labs' reports have been referenced in American city and state-level legislation regarding caste.) The passage was taken from their website and representative of their rhetoric—it was sensationalized and charged and prioritized narrative over factual accuracy. Group B was presented with a short passage describing *varna* (social class) and *jati* (subcaste) as they are understood in their original Hindu form and an acknowledgment about how these concepts were contorted into the caste system during the British colonial era. The goal was to represent an academically grounded and balanced perspective of theology versus sociopolitical factors.

Both groups were then presented with the following scenario:

Raj Kumar applied to an elite East Coast university in Fall 2022. During the application process, he was interviewed by an admissions officer, Anand Prakash. Ultimately, Raj's application was rejected.

Both the admissions officer and the applicant have Hindu-sounding names, but they are fairly generic—nothing in them indicates a particular caste. Even so, the names were reversed between respondents to avoid any potential undetected clues. This was the *only* information provided to the participants.

Participants were then asked a series of questions to ascertain the extent to which they perceived casteism (caste-based discrimination) in the admissions process and the decision. The participants who had read the Equality Labs passage were significantly more likely to perceive microaggressions, perceived harm, and assumptions of caste-based bias compared to the other group.

We then assessed the influence of the caste sensitivity essay from Equality Labs on participants' assumptions about Hindus' racist attitudes or their willingness to punish the fictional college administrator. The results indicated a significant effect on both counts, so much so that we determined that this particular content could generate broader prejudices against the Hindu American community, including creating a false "intuition" that Hindus are inherently racist.

All from reading about 180 words. Not a full sensitivity training. Kind of astonishing right?

Wait, it gets wilder!

In the next part of the study, we adapted statements made by Adolf Hitler, replacing "Jew" with "Brahmin" (the caste group depicted by Equality Labs as the oppressors). Participants who read the Equality Labs passage were *significantly* more likely to endorse Hitler's demonizing statements, shifted to Brahmins. (We didn't reveal the original source of the statements.) The group that read the Equality Labs passage were markedly more likely to agree that Brahmins were "parasites," "viruses," and "the devil personified."

Bear in mind that the prevalence and impact of caste-based discrimination in the U.S. is highly understudied and mostly speculative. Equality Labs' frequently cited report was strongly critiqued by the Carnegie Endowment for International Peace and others for its obvious methodological flaws, including unrepresentative sampling and an over-reliance on unverified self-reported experiences. Meanwhile, thorough research conducted by the Pew Research Center indicates that few American-born Hindus identify strongly with caste.

With all of that as context, it is disheartening to see that Equality Labs continues to be hired across the University of California college system to conduct caste sensitivity training. Equally disturbing is the fact that the organization's demonstrably flawed research continues to be cited as evidence of rampant caste-based discrimination in the U.S. by American politicians and scholars in the name of anti-discrimination.

It's staggering to recognize the powerful and pervasive impact of public pedagogy.

Public pedagogy is one mechanism that transmits these chronic stereotypes about Hinduism, not only within American society, but across the globe to Indian Hindus who view American democracy and progressive discourse as the gold standard against which all progressive discourse about democracy is measured and understood and are eager to promote equity and to be upstanding citizens themselves. (This is particularly true for the English-speaking crowd.)

Figure 16. I made this meme from the Netflix show *Indian Matchmaking* a few years ago. The woman in the frame is an American citizen.

America has long invested in marketing herself as an aspirational brand. Don't get me wrong— there are a lot of wonderful, aspirational things about this country! But I think we can agree that there is a difference between admiring the positive aspects of American society and importing Americanness as *the* right way to be a good society.

If Americanness is seen and exported in this way, and a certain segment of Indian Hindus want to essentially be American, then "Kill the Hindu, Save the American" is exported to India, the womb of Hinduism. What may surprise some readers is that this is transmitted through both *progressive* and *conservative* Western voices and language. Being American, even in

India, means viewing Hinduism through the assumptions we have been reading about all throughout this book. It means suppressing or erasing internal Hinduness, unlocking a whole new level of cultural genocide. This, then informs everything about how the functioning of Indian democracy is perceived and narrated by the Indians who have internalized this messaging. This is what they perceive and narrate when Indian democracy comes into contact with Hinduness (or "Hindutva" in Sanskrit). And it is *this* set of voices—the progressive, urban, educated, English-speaking ones—that are referenced as the only reliable Hindu voices to narrate back to the West.

The endogenous cycle, or circular logic, is complete.

Entertainment media can sometimes make distant lives feel closer, sparking empathy for people we may never meet. But for many Hindus in America, how they are depicted in television and film, and how they are referenced in the classroom, have too often done the opposite, distorting or erasing what gives our traditions meaning. In the stories of Sita, Madhav, Dushyant, and Chandini, we see both sides of that coin: how screens and schools can plant false ideas and how real-life relationships with neighbors, classmates, or colleagues can offer the chance to replace them with understanding.

Sita, Madhav, Dushyant, and Chandini: What We See, What We Live

It is midweek when I drive to meet Sita and her family. She is home from UCLA for a short visit, taking a break from the intense rhythm of her pre-med studies. Their home is warm in the way that only a lived-in family home can be—framed photographs along the walls, soft chatter from the kitchen, and the smells of spices blooming in hot oil. Her mother and two younger siblings greet me first. Soon the table is set. It is a traditional South Indian meal—fluffy white rice, steaming *sambar* (a lentil stew), tangy *rasam* (a spiced tamarind broth), vegetable curry, cool yogurt, and crisp *appalam* (thin lentil wafers). I am invited to eat, but we've agreed to speak one-on-one, so Sita and I settle into a quieter room off to the side.

She tells me she watched *Never Have I Ever* (a Netflix coming-of-age comedy about a Hindu American teenager in California) for the drama, "but Devi ..." She pauses, searching for the right words. "She just hated her culture the entire time. I get that some people feel that way, but the way they did it—it felt demeaning. It didn't feel like representation. If anything, it was the opposite." She explains that Devi is supposed to be Tamilian, from the same South Indian state as her own family, but she never recognized herself in the portrayal. "At the end she does one dance, and that's supposed to be her embracing her identity. But that's such a superficial part of being Indian—or Hindu. They never showed her engaging with anything Hindu at all."

As she talks, I'm aware of the layers here. Sita isn't critiquing the show as an academic might; she's speaking as someone whose peers will watch it and believe it is authentic. She is watching as a member of the audience, yes, but also as a participant in the ongoing, unspoken curriculum about who Hindus are. The show becomes a kind of public pedagogy, delivering its own lessons about which aspects of our identities are worth keeping and which can be dismissed.

Later, her father Madhav joins me in the same small room. His stories take a different turn, away from the screen and into the neighborhood. When his mother passed away, he told a few close neighbors why he would be traveling to India. One, a schoolteacher, became curious about the rituals. "For them, it is very different," he says. "They did not understand that even after your mother passes away, you still have responsibilities for her for so many days." He explains how he walked the neighbor through the process—the significance of each ritual, the sense of duty to the one who has gone, and the community's role. "It was an eye-opener for them. They were very curious. But these conversations only happen one-on-one. It cannot be an educational session or anything like that. Only when you know someone well."

His words stay with me because they remind me that public pedagogy isn't always public in the conventional sense. Sometimes it is a neighbor's quiet question, asked in trust, answered over a fence or at a kitchen table. It is still teaching, but of the kind that travels slowly, person to person, shaping how people see us in the most intimate of ways.

A few days later, I visit another family's home, this time in the South Bay. As I settle into Dushyant's living room, his wife brings us tea, and his daughters (in their early 20s) join us briefly before moving to another part of the house. We share slices of cake, and the conversation turns toward representation. "Idol worship—people here cannot digest it," he says matter-of-factly. "If you read the comments online, you'll see. They think converting Hindus is saving us from hell." He laughs a little, but it's a laugh tinged with resignation. "Some of our customs are not well respected. And it's not new.

I remember watching *Indiana Jones* long ago and thinking, 'This is how you portray us?'"

I think about the persistence of those images—how a film made decades ago can still frame how people imagine Hinduism. The screen becomes a textbook of its own, carrying caricatures forward long after the credits roll. The lesson is rarely subtle: Hinduism is strange, primitive, and dangerous. And yet those who learn it often don't even realize they've been taught.

On my last day in California, I meet with Chandini, a 20-something professional, in a hotel lobby in downtown San Francisco. Divya, my host from the East Bay, has told me that I must make a point of meeting Chandini, whom she has known through the local Hindu American community for years. (Chandini grew up near Pammi's family.) The lobby hums with the sounds of luggage wheels, phone calls, and clinking coffee cups. We discover we were in the same sorority—different chapters, different decades—but the familiarity makes us both laugh. Chandini's school memories of Hinduism are sparse: a few pages in sixth-grade world history, mostly about the caste system. Teachers would turn to her for answers she didn't have. "I knew some things culturally, but not the historical parts," she said. Then, in the middle of the unit, someone decided the class should do a dance to 'Jai Ho' from *Slumdog Millionaire*. They asked her to choreograph it. "It had nothing to do with the unit. So bizarre."

When they covered the caste system, classmates asked her outright which one she belonged to. She had never once discussed caste with her family. "I told them, 'I don't know. It's not relevant.' But as a sixth grader, I just went along with it," she said. "The way she tells it, the moment is almost casual. But

I can see how the lesson didn't end when the teacher closed the book. The framing of Hinduism in the classroom spilled into the social life of the students. They carried it into their interactions with her, expecting her to confirm their new "knowledge."

By the end of the week, I realize that none of these conversations were explicitly about public pedagogy, and yet every one of them was. Whether through a scripted Netflix show, the curiosity of a neighbor, the framing of a blockbuster film, or a sixth-grade history lesson that jumps from caste to *Slumdog Millionaire*, the messages about Hindus and Hinduism are constant. They are absorbed in classrooms and living rooms, in one-on-one conversations and mass media. And while the Hindu experience of being religious in the U.S. is distinct from that of other groups, the work of noticing how we are being taught about ourselves—often by others—feels urgently familiar.

CHAPTER SEVEN

Striving: Hindu American Advocacy in American Public Education

The Hindu framework conceptualizes time differently than the way most Americans think about it. In the West, time is conceptualized as a line, moving from past and present to future, marching ever forward. For Hindus, time is spherical, cyclical. Patterns emerge and re-emerge, insights are uncovered, covered, and rediscovered, like the waves pouring onto a beach, only to be pulled back from the shore and swallowed up into the ocean again. The waves and the tides are in conversation with the moon, Chandra, who signifies the mind and emotions.

Back in Chapter Two, I promised we'd talk about a significant Hindu visitor from India to the U.S. at the end of the 19th century.

That visitor was Swami Vivekananda!

Concerned with how Hinduism was being portrayed in the West, when Swami Vivekananda heard about the First Parliament of the World's Religions, which was planned as part of the World's Columbian Exposition in Chicago, he saw an important opportunity. First, he recognized that it would provide an opportunity to counter colonial-era distortions about Hinduism. It would also allow him to promote an alternate vision to unity, one that came from a Hindu perspective—unity in diversity. Securing funding from the Raja of Ramnad and other patrons, he arrived in the U.S. several months before the Parliament would convene. He traveled to Boston, where he met Harvard professor John Henry Wright. Wright was impressed by the young Swami's thoughts on Hindu philosophy. Wright provided him with the credentials and sponsorship to apply to speak at the conference. (Wright's now famous letter to the Parliament chairman said, "To ask you, Reverend Chairman, for credentials for this man is like asking you to give the sun permission to shine.")

Swami Vivekananda was a media sensation. "Sisters and Brothers of America," he began in his famous opening speech at the Parliament. He delivered several more addresses throughout the Parliament. In his closing address, he stated, "The Parliament has proved to the world that holiness, purity and charity are not the exclusive possessions of any church in the world, and that every system has produced men and women of the most exalted character."

Unsurprisingly, not all of late 19th-century American society welcomed him. Here was a brown, enrobed guru from an exotic tradition visiting from a far-off colonized land … and he was charismatic! Still, he had a growing fan base amongst Americans.

After making waves in Chicago, Swami Vivekananda traveled across the U.S. for two years lecturing and teaching to both public audiences and private groups. He consistently emphasized pluralism, open-mindedness, and liberty as core tenets of Hinduism and a thriving society. "Each system has its own truths, and we must learn to recognize them, and also to see the truth in others' systems," he shared with a New York audience in January 1896.

Swami Vivekananda was well-spoken, measured, and charismatic, and his presence challenged the American public's imagination about Hinduism, which had long been portrayed, as we know, as superstitious and backward. Returning to the U.S. for a second tour in 1900, he spoke about a new vision of true religious freedom in San Francisco, "We Hindus have taught the world that it is not necessary that there should be only one system of ethics or one system of metaphysics. Systems are many, because men are many; each man should have that which is most suited to him."

While Ralph Waldo Emerson and Henry David Thoreau had immersed themselves in Hindu scriptures and written with deep appreciation for Hindu philosophy well before Swami Vivekananda's visit, here was an actual practicing Hindu guru on American land.

> The sentences of the Indian sages
> ... are as grand as the mountains,
> and as pure as the snow.
>
> – Ralph Waldo Emerson

Swami Vivekananda's visit and his message are not just an important part of Hindu history, they are a part of Hindu *American* history. And, yet, we must remember not to rely solely on "heroes and holidays" to represent Hindu American history. There is so much more to our story, embedded in the lives of everyday Hindu Americans, as we've seen throughout these pages.

The Opportunity of K-12 Education

Through my work in the community (and, of course, social media), I have had the opportunity to observe how scholars in higher education are often complicit in actively and diligently misrepresenting Hinduism and Hindu Americans. Where academia falls short and can be tone deaf and even look down upon communities … public school teachers offer something completely different. The connection between immigrant communities and public school educators has only grown stronger over the past century. Public school exists at a very local level, at the heart of community, and public school teachers are a part of the communities in which they teach. Across the country, we've seen examples of how schools, when they're doing things right, listen skillfully and compassionately and thoughtfully at the classroom level, at the school level, at the district level, to immigrant communities. They want to understand their experiences, to do right by the families they serve and incorporate those understandings into how they teach. (Think back to Yagnee's teacher sharing the video of her testimony with the entire class, and the impact this had on Yagnee and on her classmates.)

K-12 public school classrooms can breathe and serve in ways that academia is not always designed for or open to. It is not always the case, of course, that this works out the way we want it to every time. There is a lot to improve and not every single interaction between communities and schools is positive. But many are. This is more than a possibility—these are the strongest threads of our society. This is exactly how we have built unity out of diversity.

In fact, I find it quite curious when academics and journalists take it upon themselves to describe the Hindu Americans who have testified before the California Department of Education and have engaged in advocating with schools as some kind of double agents; they accuse immigrant parents from India of using their children like puppets to advance some kind of anti-democratic agenda. Every single young person I interviewed, when I presented them with this conspiracy theory, was genuinely surprised by it. Some even chuckled. In fact, they all made it very clear that they saw their participation as their civic responsibility as members of American society.

The fact is, there is nothing more emblematic of American democracy than showing up to have your voice heard and your perspective represented. Ours is a participatory democracy and American public education not only teaches that—it models it. Public schools represent the most significant, most present government institution in the lives of immigrant communities. About one in four of all school aged children in the U.S. is a second-generation American—meaning they have at least one immigrant parent. About two out of every three Hindu Americans are immigrants. Hindu Americans are one of the youngest immigrant communities in the country; we have a small second generation and an even smaller third generation. But we will start to see the birth of a fourth generation of Hindu Americans in the next decade—the great-grandchildren of those first Hindus who arrived here in the 1960s and 1970s. And of course, there are Hindu Americans, like the late Yvette Rosser, who were born in another tradition here in the U.S. and found that their spiritual longing led them there naturally.

Advocacy Works

Because of Hindu American advocacy, Aryan Invasion Theory (AIT) is now represented with greater accuracy in American textbooks, at least in some versions. In the Savvas *Ancient Civilizations Grade 6* textbook, the theory is referenced under the label "Aryan migration," which states that: "About 1500 BCE, a group of people called Aryans migrated into the Indian subcontinent ... Scholars believe these people came from Central Asia and entered India through the Hindu Kush mountains."

While the term "invasion" is not explicitly used in this textbook, the content follows the narrative framework of AIT: a foreign group (Aryans) arrived from outside India and significantly shaped Indian society. This narrative often implicitly supports the invasion/migration hypothesis, especially when framed as the origin of Vedic culture or caste. In contrast, California's 2016 History–Social Science Framework takes a more cautious stance. It refers to "debates" around the Aryan migration/invasion theory and encourages teachers to engage students with multiple perspectives, including Indigenous viewpoints that challenge the notion of an external origin for Vedic culture. The Framework states "Students should learn that while many scholars have supported the Aryan migration theory, others have criticized it as lacking sufficient evidence or reflecting colonial biases."

So, while some textbooks continue to teach AIT or variants of it, more recent frameworks like California's aim to encourage critical thinking and expose students to alternative theories. This shift is partly in response to advocacy from Hindu American scholars and community groups who argue that AIT perpetuates colonial-era narratives.

There is great possibility in continuing to build strong connections between public school educators and Hindu American communities. There is great possibility in engaging American-born Hindus as mediators and participants and sociocultural translators in these spaces. There isn't one singular Hindu American perspective, and we are not all experts on religion. In fact, our tradition and community are inherently pluralist—a federation, like Vayu (who made the dinosaur analogy back in Chapter Five) said—which might make this appear even more elusive. But I believe we can figure it out.

Unity in diversity, remember?

Sitting together to understand each other, to listen to one another, offers important insight. When we think about something like culturally sustaining pedagogies, we can recognize that teaching about Hinduism in our schools means more than recognizing the accomplishments and contributions of Hinduism and Hindu society. It means representing Hinduism as a coherent philosophy and embodied practice and a unique, ethical worldview. It means imagining Sanātana Dharma not only as a world religion, but as a tradition of inquiry that exists in the U.S. and is part of the pulse of our democracy.

What Comes Next?

You've made it this far in this strange and complicated story about how and why Hinduism and Hindus are represented the way they are by American public schools. Hopefully, by sharing it in the context of other communities' struggles and successes, it has pointed us in the direction of possibility and hope. That is my intention.

But possibility and hope are obviously not enough! How do we continue to build on the ongoing successes of the past? If Hinduism and Hindus are represented as irrational, immoral, and unconcerned with civic participation—and, therefore, incompatible with American democracy—what can we do collectively and as individuals to flip the script?

The first thing is to keep educating ourselves.

If you are a parent, student, or educator (Hindu or otherwise!) and you had never really heard about or paid attention to how Hinduism is represented in our public schools, go online and check out the middle school and high school standards for your state that pertain to Hinduism, Ancient India, world religions, South Asian Studies. You might have to do a little digging, but thankfully it is probably all online on your state's department of education website. Then see if you can get a copy of the textbooks and other curricular materials used by your school or district that correlate with those standards. That might involve a skillfully worded phone call or email. (Remember, the key to all of this is thoughtful and meaningful relationship building between educators and parents.) As you go through those standards and texts, keep in mind what you've learned here as a kind of decoder ring to unlock the "hidden curriculum" of the text.

Parents and other community advocates, I would advise against marking up these materials and showing up in a meeting with a teacher or superintendent with line item "corrections." Remember, the teachers and superintendents don't determine what goes into textbooks.

Remember that the purpose of school is not just as a place for children to be taught "the facts" but how to think critically about what one reads and to navigate, discuss, and deconstruct narratives generatively and not simply argumentatively. Hopefully this book has demonstrated how much more there is to the public education project.

On that note, if you are a parent or student or advocate who was already aware of these misrepresentations and biases, but you didn't have a deeper understanding of the American educational project, continue to educate yourself with these histories, perspectives, and approaches. Familiarize yourself with the advocacy work of other communities. Learn about the Little Rock Nine, Ruby Bridges, Jo Ann Allen Boyce, and the thousands of children who bravely desegregated schools across the country, often in the face of violent protests. Discover how other communities, since the Civil Rights Era, have advocated for how they are represented and what it took to be successful. Dig past the current landscape of social activism into the history of civil rights movements and approaches from generations ago. Use this context to inform your internal perspective, your relationship building, your advocacy work, and how you talk with your family and community about these matters.

Beyond history, learn about the approaches to teaching used in American schools and the harms and possibilities they afford. For instance, countless Hindu American students report that their teachers use role-play to "enact" the caste system and how this leads to harmful negative impressions about Hindu American students from their peers. Role-play is a powerful teaching tool, as it creates an impression that nestles into the mind and psyche much more vividly than simply reading about something in a textbook. It becomes a personal experience that is hard to forget or dismiss. Find out if your local school is doing this kind of role-play; have a conversation with teachers about how this impacts children, perhaps share a summary of the Social Perceptions Lab experiment on caste, and explore alternate uses of role-play in teaching about Hinduism and Hindus.

Don't be disproportionately focused on correcting textbooks. Yes, it is important to critically examine authoritative educational materials. They do hold power. But gifted teachers can turn anything into a teaching tool— a textbook can be turned into the *object* of study rather than passively consumed as the source of "correct" information. But also remember that the conversation about textbooks first began in the 19th century. Textbooks are still in use, but there are so many other ways to tackle these issues. We cannot be stuck solving 20th-century problems with 20th-century solutions! There are things that we can do collectively as a community of Hindu American educators, parents, and students, like creating print and digital resources that engage both content and teaching approaches, which teachers and students can easily reference and apply. (I recommend checking out the Facing History & Ourselves website for a great model.) As individuals, we can become more actively engaged in school community leadership by joining the PTA, attending school board meetings, and educating ourselves on the broad spectrum of challenges and opportunities in schools today.

This is also an important time to re-envision our Hindu "Sunday schools," including reviewing curriculum updates, teacher education, and how well these programs address the lives of second, third, and even fourth generation Hindu American children and families. The same goes for the burgeoning space of Hindu American home schooling; it is vital that we remember that these programs—and our children—don't exist in a bubble. How can we think about these home-school and public-school alternative models as a part of the fabric of American society building, rather than simply an antidote or alternative to the perceived and real ills of public school? How can we design Hindu American education to be in conversation with the challenges and opportunities of American democratic society?

If you're a teacher, I hope that you've enjoyed and related to this book and the significant role that you play in the lives of so many communities. I hope that I have sufficiently conveyed how much I really appreciate and honor the teacher force and what you do. Whether or not you have Hindu students in your classroom, I hope you feel inspired to reflect and examine what is taught in your school or district. There are a lot of very cool curricula you can design from here that goes beyond textbooks and aligns with so many of the other standards you are expected to teach in terms of critical thinking and research skills in social studies, media studies, and language! You could have your students examine social media for the themes that emerged out of this book, the main one, of course, being that Hinduism is at odds with democracy. You could have students follow other things that are happening in the world. Students could conduct an analysis of mainstream journalism representations or popular entertainment. Once you see these themes, you can't unsee them, and the teaching possibilities are kind of endless. Do what teachers do best! Innovate, hack, experiment, bring new approaches to life! Share what you've learned here and your innovations with your teachers' networks and create intergroup dialogue in your school communities.

Whatever you decide to do, I hope that you don't just let what you've learned sit in a comfortable spot in your head or become a social media post.

American education and democracy are in another powerful and historical moment of inflection during what is described as a polycrisis. The fallout from the pandemic, the pervasiveness of social media, rising environmental concerns, social division, and the arrival and meteoric growth of generative AI have educators, politicians, thought leaders … nearly everyone asking foundational questions about how to redesign our public institutions and pivot our processes to respond not only to the present moment but prepare our descendants for futures that are far beyond our view. Educators and parents are asking, yet again, what is the purpose of education? What are we educating for? What does it mean and what does it take to provide responsible, meaningful education in a constantly shifting landscape?

In my 20-plus years in the field of public education, I have seen that some of the best innovation comes out of our K-12 classrooms. It may not make it into academic journals or newspaper headlines, but I think there's a quiet and great possibility here. We already see it in the responsiveness, nimbleness, and ingenuity of K-12 teachers in the face of generative AI. Really thoughtful, community facing innovation emerges from our schools, at the grassroots level, either in response to context or as thought leaders that are moving and thinking ahead of the context. I think that that's really, really exciting. And I think that Hindu Americans and Hinduism have a really interesting role to play in all of that, and not just because so many Hindu Americans work in tech!

I see this moment of disruption as an opportunity for a grand shift in how Hinduism and Hindu Americans are perceived as contributors to the experiment of American democracy, as opposed to its foil. Hinduism is rich with powerful concepts and practices of pluralism and non-duality that are inherently democratic and inclusive. Our tradition teaches us about the limitations of a purely material relationship with the world, of the necessity of self-knowledge and self-discipline, of understanding our minds, and offers tools to navigate the moral dilemmas we all face regularly as human beings and as a society. Improving how Hindu Americans and our values and worldviews are perceived is not just about our community; it is one more step in helping *all* minority communities be valued and understood. There are so many interesting perspectives that we all have to offer to our *Karma Bhumi*—our land of action.

Fall 1987

"Why don't you tell us about *your* India?"

Now is my moment. I've never spoken up before in school. Certainly, never spoken out like *that*.

I imagine everyone's eyes on me, and as my words tumble out, I can hear my own voice from inside my head as I share that yes, there are parts of India that look like those pictures, but that's not all there is. There are also beautiful homes and vibrant villages and bustling cities.

The next day, I bring in photographs from India, of my grandparents' home, of me with my cousins and aunts and uncles. Mr. Gross makes time during class for me to share them with everyone. Apart from my close friends, I have never shared this part of my life— photographs of me in India— with my classmates before, and we have been in school together since kindergarten. I talk about how the homes I have stayed in are comfortable and there is so much love. Some homes are smaller, but they are all kept clean. And while life there is different from our lives here, it is full of joy and family and laughter and the most delicious food. I describe traveling by bus in the scorching heat to play in waterfalls with my cousins and visiting ancient temples that you can't even imagine here in America.

Fall 1991

Uma is in Mr. Gross's class, and they have just reached the same infamous chapter.

"You're Indu's sister, right?"

"Yeah."

"Why don't *you* teach us about India?"

ENDNOTES

1   Frances K. Pohl, *Framing America: A Social History of American Art*, 3rd ed. (Thames & Hudson, 2012), pp. 103–105.

2   Vamsee Juluri, *Rearming Hinduism: Nature, Hinduphobia, and the Return of Indian Intelligence* (Westland Ltd., 2015), pp. 103–105.

3   This phrase comes from the Preamble to the United States Constitution, which establishes the purpose of the Constitution: to create a stronger, more unified nation than that framed by the Articles of Confederation, the Constitution's predecessor. American students typically study the Preamble in middle or high school.

4   a. Sriraj Aiyer, Wing Yan (Florence) Chan, Gilad Feldman, "Outcome Bias in Evaluations of Ethical Decisions: Replication and Extensions of Gino, Moore, and Bazerman (2009)," *Collabra: Psychology* 10, no. 1 (16 January 2024): 126266, https://doi.org/10.1525/collabra.126266.

    b. A. Gaboriaud, F. Gautheron, J.-C. Quinton, and A. Smeding, "The Effects of Intent, Outcome, and Causality on Moral Judgments and Decision Processes," *Psychologica Belgica* 62, no. 1 (2022): 218–229.

5   a. B. Orobio de Castro, J. W. Veerman, W. Koops, J. D. Bosch, and H. Monshouwer, "Hostile Attribution and Aggressive Behavior: A Meta-Analysis," *Child Development* 73, no. 3 (2002): 916–934, https://doi.org/10.1111/1467-8624.00447.

    b. K. A. Dodge, P. S. Malone, J. E. Lansford, E. Sorbring, A. T. Skinner, S. Tapanya, L. M. U. Tirado, A. Zelli, L. P. Alampay, S. M. Al-Hassan, D. Bacchini, A. S. Bombi, M. H. Bornstein, L. Chang, K. Deater-Deckard, L. Di Giunta, P. Oburu, and C. Pastorelli, "Hostile Attributional Bias and Aggressive Behavior in Global Context," *Proceedings of the National Academy of Sciences U.S.A.* 112, no. 30 (2015): 9310–9315, https://doi.org/10.1073/pnas.1418572112.

6   a. F. Cushman, R. Sheketoff, S. Wharton, and S. Carey, "The Development of Intent-Based Moral Judgment," *Cognition* 127, no. 1 (2013): 6–21, https://doi.org/10.1016/j.cognition.2012.11.008.

b. J. Li, L. Zhu, and Q. Wang, "The Development of Intent-Based Moral Judgment and Moral Behavior: Cultural Differences," *International Journal of Behavioral Development* 44, no. 2 (2020), pp. 133–141, https://doi.org/10.1177/0165025419885024.

7   a. M. Białek and W. De Neys, "Dual-Process Theory and Moral Decision-Making: A Critical Review," *Frontiers in Psychology* 7 (2016): 2202, https://doi.org/10.3389/fpsyg.2016.02202.

b. Y. Hu, L. Li, and F. Yu, "Intention Affects Fairness Processing: Evidence from Behavior and Neuroimaging," *Frontiers in Neuroscience* 17 (2023): 1128638, https://doi.org/10.3389/fnins.2023.1128638.

c. S. S. Wiltermuth, B. Monin, and R. M. Chow, "The Role of Intent in Moral Judgments of Purity Violations," *Journal of Experimental Social Psychology* 90 (2020): 104003, https://doi.org/10.1016/j.jesp.2020.104003.

8   Yagnee's mother, Purvi, later tells me that Yagnee means "one who is the recipient of all the offerings into the Yagna (divine fire)."

9   Note: I did not feel it was appropriate to approach Purvi Makwana for an interview at the time. This citation is pulled from a newspaper article.

10   https://thefederal.com/international/indian-american-dalit-activist-milind-makwana-dies-of-heart-attack/?infinitescroll=1.

11   David Tyack and Larry Cuban, *Tinkering Toward Utopia: A Century of Public School Reform* (Harvard University Press, 1995).

12   Samuel Bowles and Herbert Gintis, *Schooling in Capitalist America: Educational Reform and the Contradictions of Economic Life* (Basic Books, 1976).

13   William J. Reese, *America's Public Schools: From the Common School to "No Child Left Behind"* (Johns Hopkins University Press, 2005).

14   David Tyack and Larry Cuban, *Tinkering Toward Utopia: A Century of Public School Reform* (Harvard University Press, 1995), pp. 192–193.

15   Joel Spring, *The American School: A Global Context from the Puritans to the Trump Era* (Routledge, 2021).

16   a. Raymond E. Callahan, *Education and the Cult of Efficiency: A Study of the Social Forces That Have Shaped the Administration of the Public Schools* (University of Chicago Press, 1962).

b. Herbert M. Kliebard, *The Struggle for the American Curriculum, 1893–1958* (Routledge, 1986).

c. David B. Tyack, *The One Best System: A History of American Urban Education* (Harvard University Press, 1974).

17   Joel Spring, *The American School: A Global Context from the Puritans to the Trump Era* (Routledge, 2021).

18   Ivan Illich, *Deschooling Society* (Harper & Row, 1971).

19   John Dewey, *Democracy and Education: An Introduction to the Philosophy of Education* (Macmillan, 1916).

20   Christine E. Sleeter, "Why Is There Learning Disabilities? A Critical Analysis of the Birth of the Field in Its Social Context," *Teachers College Record* 95, no. 2 (1993), pp. 210–237.

21   Beth A. Ferri and David J. Connor, *Reading Resistance: Discourses of Exclusion in Desegregation and Inclusion Debates* (Peter Lang, 2006).

22   Carl F. Kaestle, *Pillars of the Republic: Common Schools and American Society, 1780–1860* (Hill and Wang, 1983).

23   David Nasaw, *Schooled to Order: A Social History of Public Schooling in the United States* (Oxford University Press, 1979).

24   Jurgen Herbst, *From Religion to Politics: Debates and Conflicts about Religion in American Public Schools* (University of Wisconsin Press, 1996).

25   James D. Anderson, *The Education of Blacks in the South, 1860–1935* (University of North Carolina Press, 1988).

26   Wayne J. Urban and Jennings L. Wagoner Jr., *American Education: A History* (Routledge, 2020), esp. chapters on Mann and the 19th-century reforms.

27   Carl F. Kaestle, *Pillars of the Republic: Common Schools and American Society, 1780–1860* (Hill and Wang, 1983), pp. 118–123.

28   David Tyack and Elisabeth Hansot, *Managers of Virtue: Public School Leadership in America, 1820–1980* (Basic Books, 1982), p. 20.

29   a. David Tyack and Elisabeth Hansot, *Managers of Virtue: Public School Leadership in America, 1820–1980* (Basic Books, 1982).

b. Amy Gutmann, *Democratic Education* (Princeton University Press, 1987).

30   William J. Reese, *America's Public Schools: From the Common School to "No Child Left Behind"* (Johns Hopkins University Press, 2005), p. 30.

31   Lawrence A. Cremin, *American Education: The National Experience, 1783–1876* (New York: Harper & Row, 1980), p. 122.

32   David Tyack and Thomas James, *Law and the Shaping of Public Education, 1785–1954* (University of Wisconsin Press, 1987), p. 26.

33   Lawrence A. Cremin, *American Education: The National Experience, 1783–1876* (Harper & Row, 1980), pp. 180–183.

34   *Carlisle Indian School Digital Resource Center*, "'Kill the Indian in him, and save the man,'" accessed December 1, 2025, carlisleindian.dickinson.edu/teach/kill-indian-him-and-save-man-r-h-pratt-education-native-americans.

35   While Kipling wrote extensively about India and Hindus, his representations of Hindus were heavily influenced by colonial tropes and agendas.

36　Rudyard Kipling, "The White Man's Burden: The United States and the Philippine Islands," *McClure's Magazine*, February 1899.

37　John A. Nietz, *Old Textbooks* (University of Pittsburgh Press, 1961), p. 4.

38　John A. Nietz, *Old Textbooks: Spelling, Grammar, Reading, Arithmetic, Geography, American History, Civil Government, Physiology, Penmanship, Art, Music, as Taught in the Common Schools from Colonial Days to 1900* (University of Pittsburgh Press, 1961), pp. 196–200.

39　I am not endorsing Altman's conceptualization of Hinduism, in this book or in his other work, but if the reader is interested in understanding more about the context of how Hinduism was represented in schoolbooks during that era, Chapter Three of *Heathen, Hindoo, Hindu* is worth a read.

40　Michael J. Altman, *Heathen, Hindoo, Hindu* (Oxford University Press, 2017), pp. 58–59.

41　W. L. Stuart, "Calcutta, the City of Palaces," *Harper's New Monthly Magazine* 34, no. 201 (1867): 302–303, reproduced in M. J. Altman, *Heathen, Hindoo, Hindu: American Representations of India* (Oxford University Press, 2017).

42　S. Augustus Mitchell, *Mitchell's School Geography: A System of Modern Geography, Comprising a Description of the Present State of the World and Its Grand Divisions: North America, South America, Europe, Asia, Africa, and Oceanica* (1867), illustrated engraving reproduced in M. J. Altman, *Heathen, Hindoo, Hindu: American Representations of India, 1721–1893* (Oxford University Press, 2017), p. 55.

43　David Kopf, "A Macrohistoriographical Essay on the Idea of East and West from Herodotus to Edward Said," *Comparative Civilizations Review* 15, no. 15 (1986), pp. 22–42.

44　S. Augustus Mitchell, *Mitchell's School Geography: A System of Modern Geography, Comprising a Description of the Present State of the World and Its Grand Divisions: North America, South America, Europe, Asia, Africa, and Oceanica* (Philadelphia, PA: Cowperthwait, Desilver & Butler, 1867).

45　S. Town and N. M. Holbrook, *The Progressive Third Reader: For Public and Private Schools: Containing the Elementary Principles of Elocution, Illustrated by Examples and Exercises in Connection with Tables and Rules, and a Series of Lessons in Reading; With Original Designs and Engravings* (Boston: Sanborn, Carter, Bazin, 1857), p. 180.

46　S. Augustus Mitchell, *Mitchell's School Geography: A System of Modern Geography, Comprising a Description of the Present State of the World and Its Grand Divisions: North America, South America, Europe, Asia, Africa, and Oceanica* (Philadelphia, PA: Cowperthwait, Desilver & Butler, 1867).

47　The Goddess of Knowledge.

48 Syncreticsm is a complicated phenomenon. While some folks think of it as innovative and generative, others critique it as a result (and sometimes even a subversion) of undue colonial missionary pressure to convert.

49 Timothy Matovina, *Latino Catholicism: Transformation in America's Largest Church* (Princeton: Princeton University Press, 2012), pp. 12–15.

50 Roger Daniels, *Coming to America: A History of Immigration and Ethnicity in American Life* (Harper Perennial, 2002).

51 a. Kambiz GhaneaBassiri, *A History of Islam in America: From the New World to the New World Order* (Oxford University Press, 2010).

    b. Sylviane A. Diouf, *Servants of Allah: African Muslims Enslaved in the Americas* (NYU Press, 1998).

52 Scott D. Seligman, *The First Chinese American: The Remarkable Life of Wong Chin Foo* (Hong Kong University Press, 2013).

53 Pew Research Center, "Confucianism, Taoism and Chinese Folk Religions: An Overview" (August 30, 2023), accessed December 1, 2025, pewresearch. org/religion/2023/08/30/confucianism-taoism-and-chinese-folk-religions/.

54 Honpa Hongwanji Mission of Hawaii, *Shin Buddhism in the American Context*, accessed July 26, 2025, bschawaii.org/shindharmanet/wp-content/ uploads/sites/3/2015/03/07_Chapter-Seven.pdf.

55 The Pluralism Project at Harvard University, "Buddhists in the American West," accessed July 26, 2025, pluralism.org/buddhists-in-the-american-west.

56 Don Baker, *Korean Spirituality* (University of Hawai'i Press, 2008).

57 The Pluralism Project at Harvard University, "Sikhism," accessed December 2, 2025, pluralism.org/sikhism.

58 UC Davis Punjabi Diaspora Digital Archive, "1899–1922: Arrival & Early Years," accessed December 2, 2025, pdda.lib.ucdavis.edu.

59 Nico Slate, "Bengali Harlem and the Lost Histories of South Asian America," *Journal of American History* 100, no. 3 (2013), pp. 885–886.

60 Mae M. Ngai, *Impossible Subjects: Illegal Aliens and the Making of Modern America* (Columbia University Press, 2004).

61 U.S. Immigration Commission, *The Children of Immigrants in Schools*, Vol. 2 (1911), pp. 1–15.

62 F. Cordasco, "The Children of Immigrants in the Schools: Historical Analogues of Educational Deprivation," *The Kansas Journal of Sociology* 6, no. 3 (1970), pp. 143–155, jstor.org/stable/23255064.

63 F. Cordasco, "The Children of Immigrants in the Schools: Historical Analogues of Educational Deprivation," *The Kansas Journal of Sociology* 6, no. 3 (1970), p. 149, jstor.org/stable/23255064.

64   D. Tyack, *Inside the System: The Character of Urban Schools, 1890–1940* (1974), p. 147.

65   D. Tyack, *Inside the System: The Character of Urban Schools, 1890–1940* (1974), p. 147.

66   D. Tyack, *Inside the System: The Character of Urban Schools, 1890–1940* (1974), p. 179.

67   a. U.S. Census Bureau, *Historical Statistics of the United States: Colonial Times to 1970* (U.S. Government Printing Office, 1975).

b. Roger Daniels, *Coming to America: A History of Immigration and Ethnicity in American Life* (Harper Perennial, 2002).

c. Pew Research Center, "The Religious Affiliation of U.S. Immigrants" (2013), pewresearch.org/religion/2013/05/17/the-religious-affiliation-of-us-immigrants/.

d. Hasia R. Diner, *The Jews of the United States, 1654 to 2000* (University of California Press, 2004).

e. Jay P. Dolan, *The American Catholic Experience: A History from Colonial Times to the Present* (Doubleday, 1985).

f. Timothy J. Meagher, *The Columbia Guide to Irish American History* (Columbia University Press, 2005).

g. Kambiz GhaneaBassiri, *A History of Islam in America: From the New World to the New World Order* (Oxford University Press, 2010).

h. Karen Leonard, *Making Ethnic Choices: California's Punjabi Mexican Americans* (Temple University Press, 1992).

i. Ronald Takaki, *Strangers from a Different Shore: A History of Asian Americans* (Little, Brown and Company, 1989).

j. R. Stephen Warner and Judith G. Wittner, eds., *Gatherings in Diaspora: Religious Communities and the New Immigration* (Temple University Press, 1998).

k. Joan Jensen, *Passage from India: Asian Indian Immigrants in North America* (Yale University Press, 1988).

l. Will Herberg, *Protestant, Catholic, Jew: An Essay in American Religious Sociology* (University of Chicago Press, 1955).

m. Howard M. Sachar, *A History of the Jews in America* (Vintage, 1992).

n. Charles S. Prebish, *Luminous Passage: The Practice and Study of Buddhism in America* (University of California Press, 1999).

o. Theodore Saloutos, *The Greeks in the United States* (Harvard University Press, 1964).

68   a. J. Axtell, *The Invasion Within: The Contest of Cultures in Colonial North America* (Oxford University Press, 1985).

b. A. Braude, *Radical Spirits: Spiritualism and Women's Rights in Nineteenth-Century America* (Indiana University Press, 2001).

c. K. M. Brown, *Mama Lola: A Vodou Priestess in Brooklyn* (University of California Press, 1991).

d. S. Bullock, *Revolutionary Brotherhood: Freemasonry and the Transformation of the American Social Order* (University of North Carolina Press, 1996).

e. J. Buehrens, *Universalists and Unitarians in America: A People's History* (Skinner House Books, 2011).

f. V. Deloria, Jr., *God Is Red* (Putnam, 1973).

g. J. Hostetler, *Hutterite Society* (Johns Hopkins University Press, 1974).

h. D. Kraybill, *On the Backroad to Heaven* (Johns Hopkins University Press, 2001).

i. J. L. Matory, *Black Atlantic Religion* (Princeton University Press, 2005).

j. S. Stein, *The Shaker Experience in America* (Yale University Press, 1992).

k. J. Thornton, *Africa and Africans in the Making of the Atlantic World* (Cambridge University Press, 1998).

69 a. G. Brandon, *Santería from Africa to the New World* (Indiana University Press, 1993).

b. B. Campbell, *A History of the Theosophical Movement* (University of California Press, Berkeley, 1980).

c. M. Deren, *Divine Horsemen: The Living Gods of Haiti* (McPherson, 1953).

d. J. Ghent, "Haitian Vodou in the United States," in Oxford Encyclopedia of Religion (Oxford University Press, 2018).

e. R. Peel, Mary Baker Eddy (Holt, 1966).

f. R. Romberg, Healing Dramas: Divination and Magic in Modern Puerto Rico (University of Texas Press, 2003).

g. J. Williams-Hogan, "Swedenborgians," in *Encyclopedia of American Religion* (Gale, 2015).

70 a. G. Chryssides, *Jehovah's Witnesses: Continuity and Change* (Ashgate, 2016).

b. S. Jacoby, *Freethinkers: A History of American Secularism* (Holt, 2004).

c. H. S. Lewis, *Rosicrucian Manual* (AMORC, 1918).

d. R. Numbers, *Prophetess of Health: Ellen G. White and the Origins of Seventh-Day Adventism* (Eerdmans, 2008).

e. D. Paton, *The Cultural Politics of Obeah* (Cambridge University Press, 2015).

71 a. M. Boyce, *Zoroastrians: Their Religious Beliefs and Practices* (Routledge, 2000).

b. L. Dinnerstein and D. Reimers, *Ethnic Americans: A History of Immigration* (Columbia University Press, 2009).

c. P. Doshi, "Early Jain Immigration," Journal of Jain Studies (2010).

d. P. Jain, *Dharma in America: A Short History of Hindu-Jain Diaspora* (Routledge, 2019).

e. T. Luhrmann, *The Good Parsi* (Harvard University Press, 1996).

f. M. Momen, *The Babi and Baha'i Religions* (George Ronald, 1981).

g. J. Shook, *The Oxford Handbook of Secularism* (Oxford University Press, 2017).

h. P. Smith, *An Introduction to the Bahá'í Faith* (Cambridge University Press, 2008).

i. Pew Research Center, "The Religious Composition of Immigrants to the United States"(2012, updated 2021).

72   N. Foner and R. Alba, "Immigrant Religion in the U.S. and Western Europe: Bridge or Barrier to Inclusion?," *International Migration Review* 42 (2008), p. 366.

73   K. R. Bestelmeyer, B. Yao, and C. S. H. Smith, "Own-Accent Bias and the Social Evaluation of Speech," *Language and Speech* (2024), journals.sagepub.com/doi/10.1177/0261927X241287189.

74   D. S. Storlie and S. R. Stone-Romero, "Discrimination Based on Accents: A Meta-Analytic Integration," *International Journal of Selection and Assessment* (2025), onlinelibrary.wiley.com/doi/10.1111/ijsa.12519.

75   B. Park and G. Y. Atlas, "Social Preferences and Accent Bias: Meta-Analysis of Experimental Studies," *Personality and Social Psychology Bulletin* (2022), journals.sagepub.com/doi/10.1177/01461672221130595.

76   E. H. Dąbrowska et al., "Effects of Foreign Accent on Comprehension and Processing: An fMRI Study," *Frontiers in Psychology* (2020), ncbi.nlm.nih.gov/pmc/articles/PMC6928667/.

77   J. Burn-Murdoch, "Why Accents Are Our Social Passwords," *Financial Times*, March 1, 2024, ft.com/content/2464dfdd-15fc-4bff-92c0-7f83e57819a4.

78   a. National Sexual Violence Resource Center (NSVRC), "Accent Discrimination: A Silent Barrier to Equity," NSVRC, 2023, nsvrc.org/accent-bias.

b. R. Lippi-Green, *English with an Accent: Language, Ideology, and Discrimination in the United States*, 2nd ed. (London: Routledge, 2012).

c. W. Cheung, "Accent Discrimination is a Universal Yet Socially Accepted Form of Prejudice," National Sexual Violence Resource Center, 2023.

79   This doesn't just apply to Indians and Hindus, of course. In fact, accents and American English variants of African American students and families are a

large part of the discourse that shaped and continue to shape the educational scholarship and practices we discussed in the previous chapter, including culturally relevant and sustaining pedagogies.

80   American Educational Research Association (AERA), *AERA*, 2025, aera.net.

81   AERA, *AERA by the Numbers: Divisions*, 2025, available at aera.net.

82   Jurgen Herbst, *The Once and Future School: Three Hundred and Fifty Years of American Secondary Education* (New York: Routledge, 1996), pp. 25–30.

83   James W. Fraser, *Preparing America's Teachers: A History* (New York: Teachers College Press, 2007), pp. 14–19.

84   Geraldine J. Clifford and James W. Guthrie, *Ed School: A Brief for Professional Education* (Chicago: University of Chicago Press, 1988), pp. 20–26.

85   My alma mater, Teachers College, was established in 1887 and became affiliated with Columbia University in 1893. It became the graduate school of education for Columbia University, making it the oldest and first university- affiliated teachers college in the country. It pioneered combining pedagogical training with education research and is considered the template for integrating teacher education into higher education.

86   Michael Apple, *Teachers and Texts* (New York: Routledge, 1986).

87   T. S. Popkewitz, *Title of Work* (Publisher, 1987), p. 16.

88   National Archives, "Civil Rights Act of 1964," *Milestone Documents*, accessed December 2, 2025, archives.gov/milestone-documents/civil-rights-act.

89   F. Cordasco, "The Children of Immigrants in the Schools: Historical Analogues of Educational Deprivation," *The Kansas Journal of Sociology* 6, no. 3 (1970), p. 149.

90   Django Paris and H. Samy Alim, eds., *Culturally Sustaining Pedagogies: Teaching and Learning for Justice in a Changing World* (New York: Teachers College Press, 2017), pp. 1, 95.

91   HISTORY.com Editors, "U.S. Immigration Since 1965," *History*, 2010, history.com/articles/us-immigration-since-1965.

92   Council of Indian Institutes of Technology (IITS), "About IITs," IITSSystem, accessed December 2, 2025, iitsystem.ac.in/about.

93   Roli Varma (2007). Changing Borders and Realities: Emigration of Indian Scientists and Engineers to the United States. Perspectives on Global Development and Technology, p. 542

94   Public Religion Research Institute (PRRI), *2023 PRRI Census of American Religion: County-Level Data on Religious Identity and Diversity*, PRRI Census of American Religion, 2024, prri.org/spotlight/prri-2022-american-values-atlas-religious-affiliation-updates-and-trends.

95 Exact religious breakdowns by country were not consistently tracked in early U.S. immigration data. For instance, these estimates generally assume that about 80 percent of Indian immigrants are Hindu, which aligns with India's religious demographics, which is a reasonable estimate that is used by other scholars. A similar approach was taken for calculating the remaining rows.

96 Indu Viswanathan, "Examining Anti-Hindu Bias in American Public Education: The Endogenous Cycle of Hinduphobia," *Journal of the Council for Research on Religion* 6, no. 1 (2025), 25–45, doi.org/10.26443/jcreor. v6i1.130.

97 Yvette Rosser, *Myopic Pedagogy: Prejudicial Representations of India in U.S. Social Studies Classrooms* (2018).

98 Yvette C. Rosser, "The Clandestine Curriculum: Temple of Doom in the Classroom," *Education About Asia*, Winter 2001, asianstudies.org/publications/eaa/archives/ theclandestinecurriculumtempleofdoomintheclassroom.

99 Natalia Alamdari, "Delaware Kindergarten Class That Combined Slavery with Yoga 'Unacceptable,' District Says," *The News Journal* (Delaware), February 26, 2021.

100 Michael J. Altman, *Heathen, Hindoo, Hindu: American Representations of India, 1721–1893* (New York: Oxford University Press, 2017), p. 71.

101 Network Contagion Research Institute and Rutgers University Social Perception Lab, *Instructing Animosity: How DEI Pedagogy Produces the Hostile Attribution Bias* (2024), networkcontagion.us/reports/instructing-animosity-how-dei-pedagogy-produces-the-hostile-attribution-bias/.

Acknowledgments

This book came to life because of an incredible group of people who have supported, challenged, and inspired me emotionally, spiritually, intellectually, humorously, and inadvertently.

I'd like to thank all the people who trusted me enough to interview them. Akshay, Amruta, Anirudh, Arjun, Chandini, Divya, Dushyant, Keshav, Madhav, Meghana, Nagarjuna, Pammi, Parinithi, Pranitha, Ram, Revathy, Sia, Sita, Sneha, Vaijayanthi, Vayu, and Yagnee. Your candor, sincerity, and generosity form the heart of this book.

To the late Milind ji and his family, thank you for letting me honor him in these pages.

Urmila ji, Mihir, Vasanthi, and Murali, this book would not have been possible without incredible generosity, your belief in me, and your support.

I am grateful to all of my friends who listen when I talk about these complicated things and always engage with care, curiosity, and respect. Thank you Margaret, Aley, Angel, Maria Stella, Alie, Michael, Anisha, Sumita, Donna, Naheeda, Monica, and

Katie, for encouraging me with all of your heart and for being such top-rate cheerleaders.

Thank you to my many supporters in the Hindu American and global Hindu community, for whom I feel deep care, even though I haven't met most of you in person! My interactions with you have given me so much clarity and have helped me cultivate my voice.

My deepest gratitude to my diverse community of online trolls who regularly accuse me of countless acts of treason, including (but not limited to): not being fluent in English, faking my credentials, writing too much, never having worn jeans, and being a feminist. You have taught me so much dispassion, you creative, tireless lot! What's more, you have truly inspired me to get offline and write.

To all the scholars from whose work I have learned and built my own, including those with whom I vehemently disagree, my deepest appreciation. In particular, my sincere gratitude to the late Yvette Rosser, whose contributions spring eternal in these pages. Your peerless enthusiasm never fades in my memory.

I'd like to thank my wonderful editor, Amy Tyler, who knows exactly when to push back against and when to concede to my nerdiness. Your kindness, heart, humor, and skill have made this process utterly delightful.

Thank you to all the folks at The Self Publishing Agency. What a lovely journey it has been! Thank you to Megan Williams for matching me with Amy and helping me to launch a book out into the world. And Danna Steele for playing along with so much joy and heart in designing the cover and book. What a thing!

A deep thank you to all the folks who read parts or all of my manuscript and pointed me in the right direction. MeiMei Fox, not only did you help me find the right publisher, you taught me how to bring "movie moments" into my work and unlocked a new level of writer in me. Jen Tate, with your infectious smile, my gratitude for the care with which you guided me toward telling Milind and Yagnee's story the way it lives now. Emma Seppälä, thank you for guiding me toward hope and possibility in the early days of this book concept. Sara Stevens, my old friend, what a joy it's been to gestate our books together. Thank you for being so enthusiastic and gentle at the same time. Sneha Rao, my co-conspirator, thank you for reading through this entire thing and knowing exactly what to fine tune. You all held it with such care.

My dearest Amma and Appa, Uma, Rahul and Ajay. You give me endless strength and hope and love and happiness. There aren't enough words to describe how blessed I feel. My little Bhima, you sat by my side throughout this process, providing warmth and love and protection. And to my entire, enormous family around the world and all of our ancestors, you are always with me. I chose my family well.

My deepest gratitude to my Guru, Sri Sri Ravi Shankar. You have shown me the path to my Self with such love and generosity and delight, and it has made all the difference.

About the Author

Indu Viswanathan is an educator, public scholar, and thought leader whose work brings Hindu contemplative traditions into conversation with contemporary questions in education and culture. Her research explores how learning environments shape belonging, and how cultural harmony can be nurtured through dialogue, shared stories, and reflective practice. She has taught in New York public schools and international settings, and has worked across teacher education, curriculum design, and research initiatives for more than two decades. She holds a master's degree and doctorate in education from Teachers College, Columbia University. As the co-founder of research and education initiative Understanding Hinduphobia, she has become a leading voice in national conversations about how Hinduism and the Hindu diaspora are represented in classrooms, scholarship, media, and public discourse. She also hosts the *Hindu at Heart* podcast, a conversation series with Hindus raised in America about belonging, meaning, and stewardship.

Grounded in her own practice as a Hindu, Indu is a long-time disciple of His Holiness Sri Sri Ravi Shankar, whose guidance infuses her work with a commitment to pluralism, care, and learning as a pathway to connection. She lives in Brooklyn and is the mother of two grown sons—and Bhima, her beloved rescue dog.